War&*Recovery*

A Spiritual Journey

ISBN# 978-0-9648148-4-4

By Dave Roever with Karen Crews Crump

Roever Communications, a division of Roever Foundation, Inc.
P.O. Box 136130, Fort Worth, TX 76136, 817/238-2000, daveroever.org

To Brenda

Contents

Forward

Dave Roever has never stopped being an American warrior. Committed to the enduring goodness and strength of our Nation, he has instructed, encouraged, and motivated countless young Americans. Dave has connected with the current *"greatest generation"* from high school gymnasiums to fox holes, cockpits and ship decks with a clear message of hope—real hope. Dave is not afraid to talk about the power of God and prayer in his life and "walks the talk" as he has overcome war wounds that have not deterred but strengthened him. Dave Roever is the *"real deal."* It is an honor to offer a few words of encouragement to those who will find in Dave's book, *War and Recovery—A Spiritual Journey*, the enthusiasm and inspiration that Dave has shared so humbly and courageously with so many.

—Bruce Wright
Lieutenant General, US Air Force (Retired)

About the Author

Dave Roever grew up in a loving, committed family in South Texas. The last thing on his mind was going to war. At the height of the Vietnam War, he received his draft notice. Having no desire to serve in the infantry, he joined the Navy and served as a riverboat gunner in the elite Brown Water Black Beret in Vietnam.

Eight months into his tour of duty in Vietnam, Dave was burned beyond recognition when a phosphorous grenade he was poised to throw exploded in his hand. The ordeal left him hospitalized for fourteen months, where he underwent numerous major surgeries. His survival and life are miraculous.

Today, with his humorous style, Dave Roever is enthusiastically received both nationally and internationally as a public speaker. He is a gifted communicator and speaks in a variety of settings including public schools, military installations, business conventions and churches, and is a frequent guest on national television talk shows.

In every setting, Mr. Roever's message is one of hope. Using his life as an example, he addresses issues relevant to his audience and presents concrete solutions to life's problems. Often drawing upon his war experiences of loneliness, peer pressure, disfigurement and pain, as well as life's triumphs, Dave weaves a message of courage, commitment and survival that touches and transforms those who hear him.

Thirty-four years after his injuries, the Department of the Navy corrected its oversight by awarding Dave a Purple Heart, along with several other service medals. Because of his war-time experiences of service, injury and recovery, he is uniquely qualified to speak to the needs of military personnel. He is called upon regularly to address troops on domestic military bases as well as those deployed in other locations around the globe.

In May 2005, Dave was awarded an honorary doctorate degree in recognition of his remarkable life and service.

Dave Roever is founder, chairman, and president of two non-profit corporations: Roever Evangelistic Association and Roever Foundation based in Fort Worth, Texas. Dave and his wife Brenda are co-founders of Eagles Summit Ranch where the couple trains wounded warriors, others from the U.S. military, and promising young leaders. Specific areas of focus are public speaking and emotional recovery after devastating injury.

Mr. Roever is no stranger to the war on terror. He has made six tours to the Middle East encouraging our soldiers in Afghanistan, Kuwait, Oman, Qatar, Saudi Arabia, United Arab Emirates and Iraq.

Military Awards

PURPLE HEART MEDAL

NAVY UNIT COMMENDATION RIBBON

NATIONAL DEFENSE SERVICE MEDAL

VIETNAM SERVICE MEDAL with 3 bronze stars

REPUBLIC OF VIETNAM MERITORIOUS UNIT CITATION
(Gallantry Cross Medal Color with Palm)

REPUBLIC OF VIETNAM MERITORIOUS UNIT CITATION
(Civil Actions Medal, First Class Color with Palm)

REPUBLIC OF VIETNAM CAMPAIGN MEDAL with 1960 device

★ ★ ★

Books by Dave Roever: *Welcome Home Davey, Scarred,*
Magic Fountain, and Nobody's Ever Cried for Me.

Introduction

 A S A PUBLIC SPEAKER AND RESILIENCY COACH with the Department of Defense's Comprehensive Soldier Fitness program, I do what I have done since I was injured in Vietnam. I offload my soul every time I tell my story of *Tragedy to Triumph* through faith and hope. Why would I bury the very prescriptions for success that have worked in my life? Why would I not share it with present-day warriors? It would make no sense. The spiritual man is starving to death while the soul searches for what no amount of drugs, legal or illegal, can provide.

Healing the inner man to restore the outer man is paramount. The spiritual man is healed so the physical man can be restored, and the physical man includes the brain and its functions. I do not know all the medical terms, but I see the results. The more the warrior uses his talents to offload his history of war, the better his recovery.

My own experience in *war and recovery* has been beyond successful, playing out in a lifetime of wonderment and opportunity. I have been blessed beyond degree with a wife and family. My wife and I have a marathon marriage—more than forty years and counting! No divorce. Never a moment of domestic violence. Absolutely no alcohol or drug use, much less abuse. My children and grandchildren are close to my heart and soul at all times.

Because of God's help, as a wounded warrior I have been able to overcome the unbelievable. Now I am able to pour into the lives of the wounded and challenge them to defy all odds by triumphing over their tragedies.

War and Recovery—A Spiritual Journey is a compilation of vignettes of my life and the lives of others like me.

★   ★   ★

War&*Recovery*

A Spiritual Journey

Chapter One

The Rosie Story

TWO WORDS THAT SEEM SIMILAR are *passion* and *compassion*. I am a passionate man. Anyone who knows me knows that I cannot do anything halfway. My poor wife has said to me many times, "Do you have to be so gung ho about everything?"

The answer is yes. That is just my nature. And when it comes to compassion, I do not know how to be less passionate about that than I am about anything else.

I have known suffering in my life, and it has been a hard road at times. I was burned beyond recognition in Vietnam—shot up, mutilated and almost died, but God had a plan for my life. He saw a way out, a way to use those tragedies and turn them into triumphs in other people's lives, as well as in my own.

When you realize that you cannot do life by yourself, you begin to understand that you need Someone—Someone who has passion and compassion; Someone who will carry you when no one else can. Yes, that Someone is Jesus Christ.

But in this story, that someone's name is Rosie, and he carried me.

This story can bring you hope, and it can be a springboard for a new beginning of believing that God can do a miracle in your life, too.

You'll be fine, Big Man. You'll see. You'll be fine...

It was not the choice for my life, but I ended up in Vietnam. I was there eight months and wounded twice. My second injury was devastating.

Only a few days after my first injury, which was minor, my team went back to the exact same place of the previous firefight. We were looking for bodies and trying to get an estimate of how many of the enemy we had come up against. We were looking for shell casings, rocket casings, anything that would tell us more about the enemy than what we already knew, specifically, what weapons were being used against us.

We could not do the search without getting up on the bank of the river, and that was extremely dangerous. The Viet Cong booby-trapped everything.

I was driving the boat that day, so I steered it up onto the bank and crawled into my position as forward gunner. I was standing between two .50 caliber machine guns, and I had this uncanny sense of the presence of the enemy. I knew he was there.

I felt that what I was sensing was God warning me. The enemy was there. I could not see him, hear him or smell him, but I knew he was there.

I kept my eyes on the bunker complex in front of me, and I reached down by my knee where there was a canister filled with hand grenades. I felt around for the smooth cylinder, the one that was filled with white phosphorus that burns at 5,000 degrees Fahrenheit. It only takes half of that, 2,500 degrees, to melt down the engine of a car.

That particular grenade is good for defoliation. It is good for smoke, for detonating grenades and for melting trip wires. It was the right choice. It was just what I needed to burn down the brush on the riverbank in order to have a clear view of what was there.

I pulled the pin. I drew back. And in one second, everything changed.

One second is all it takes to change a life—a single second.

Just as my left hand elevated and my right hand was passing my ear, I had no way of knowing a sniper had crosshairs trained on my head.

Squeezing off a round, he missed my head and hit my hand, exploding the grenade right beside my face. In a flash, 5,000 degrees burned off 60 pounds of flesh and half my skin. I went blind in my right eye. The force from the explosion blew my hair off, blew my ear off, blew half my face off, ripped my chest open, and I could see my heart beating. My back was on fire; skin was dripping from my arm; and my fingers and thumb were hanging by tendons. A lacerated artery was pumping the blood out of my system, and I knew it was the end for me.

I wanted my wife so badly...I did not want to die alone. I wanted her to hold me. I did not want her hurt, and I would not have taken her to war with me, but in my intense agony, I still wanted her.

I heard a loud screaming in my right ear. Was it my own voice or was it nerve damage? To try to save my life, I jumped into the river only to make a horrifying discovery—water will not extinguish burning phosphorus. My body continued to burn. With my left eye wide open, I could see my flesh floating, burning.

When I pushed to the surface to inhale, I sucked fire down into my lungs. As I exhaled, I yelled, and this is an exact, verbatim quote, registered in the hearts of all the guys who survived that day, *"God, I still believe in You!"*

After my injury, they ultimately got me to San Antonio, Texas, to Brooke Army Medical Center (BAMC, pronounced *Bam-C*). The day of my arrival at BAMC was one of the most horrendous days of my entire life.

The first thing the medical staff did, before I saw my wife, parents, or family, was to take me into a room for debridement. If you do not know what that is, it is spelled H-E-L-L.

Nothing in my life has ever hurt so badly as the day they put me into that tank of water. I had no idea what was coming. Trying to be funny, I asked, "Do I get a rubber ducky?"

Nobody laughed. They knew what I did not know. I had no more than sunk into the tank when out came the pinchers, pliers, knives, and scalpels.

Those scalpels were so sharp and those pinchers so ravaging. They would grab a chunk of burned skin and strip my body of flesh. They were literally filleting me. I am not exaggerating. Only if you have been burned, can you understand what I am saying.

I was bowed up with only my head and heels touching the bottom of the tank. I was in anguish, and the nurse did not seem to care. At least to me, it seemed that way.

I grabbed her by her hair and pulled her down into the tank with me. I had her head down, and I was trying to drown her. "I'll kill you! I'll kill you…I'll kill you! You tried to kill me… *I'll kill you!*"

The excruciating pain had sent my mind almost over the edge.

When they got her out of the tank, they said, "Well, maybe that's enough. Maybe we should stop here before he kills us all."

They took me to my bed, and just as they got me there, they said, "Oh, by the way, early in the morning we have to do this again."

All I can remember is crying out, "*No! No! No! NO!* Let me die, but please don't do this again. Why did you have to tell me? Don't tell me. Just do it, but don't tell me."

That is like a dad saying to his son, "You disobeyed me, but I am going to wait until 8:30 in the morning to punish you. Good night, big boy. Sleep well."

If he is going to get his socks whipped off him the next morning, the boy is not going to sleep. He is not going to sleep!

I knew hell was coming in the morning with a gurney draped in blue. At 8:30, right on schedule, after a sleepless night, the horror I dreaded began again. They were trying to put me onto a gurney, and they were having a hard time of it when a man walked up.

He was about 6'7" and 350 pounds of solid muscle. He was quite a specimen of humanity. When he moved his arms, cannon balls popped up. He was black, he was bald, and

22

his named was Rosie. True. *R-O-S-I-E.* A rose was tattooed on his arm.

With one hand, he gently swept the nurses and that old gurney aside. With his hands down, palms up, he pressed against the mattress. He hardly touched me when he slid those forklift arms under me. He lifted me up, and I rested my head on his giant shoulder as I looked into a face I had never seen.

He walked the long corridor to the room at the end of the hall on Ward 14A—a room with double walls to muffle the screaming. There Rosie gently put me down into the tank.

Debridement came again.

Just as I was grabbing for nurses, reaching my point of no return, and knowing I could not stand any more, I looked over, and there in the corner of the room, I saw Rosie with those giant arms folded across his chest. On that beautiful ebony face, trails of tears coursed down his cheeks and dripped from his chin. As I looked closer, I noticed his lips were moving.

Rosie was praying for me.

I felt strength come into my body, and I began to relax.

When the doctors finished, Rosie came. He put his arms down into the once-pristine water that was now filthy with decaying skin and blood. He lifted me up, and they rinsed me off and dried his arms and my body. Then they scrubbed a little to get the blood to the surface, preparing me for skin grafts.

I was in agony. I looked into Rosie's face and those eyes were staring into my soul. He turned, and I thought he would put me on the gurney, but there was no gurney for Rosie. He carried me down the hall, back to my bed.

With every step he took, he repeated words that seeped into my soul, "You'll be fine, Big Man. You'll see. You'll be fine."

"You'll be fine," he whispered softly as his tears dripped down on me, "you'll be fine."

I could not cry because I was so dehydrated. There was not enough moisture in me for tears. Rosie cried for me. And he carried me when I could not carry myself.

When he got me to my bed and pulled those forklifts out, it was with the touch of a mother's love. He pushed a little piece of hair back and then he kissed my forehead.

With those almond eyes he looked deeply into my soul, and once more he repeated, "You'll be fine, Big Man. You'll see. You'll be fine."

Rosie physically carried me, but the faithful God sustained me through all those horrendous months in the hospital. God's promises are so much a part of my life. "...I have upheld you since your birth, and have carried you since you were born. Even to your old age...I am He, I am He who

24

will sustain you. I have made you and I will carry you; I will sustain you and I will rescue you." [1]

Yes, Rosie, I'm fine. I am just fine.

[1] Isaiah 46:3-4 *Today's New International Version*

★   ★   ★

Chapter Two

You'd Do It Again

SEPTEMBER 11, 2001, CHANGED MY LIFE FOREVER. I remember sitting in front of the TV, watching as terrorists flew airplanes into tall buildings. This land for which I bled was being attacked! Screaming at the television, I cried out to God, "Don't leave me out of this war!"

Within a few weeks, I had calls from military commanders saying to me, "We are going to war, and our troops need to hear the message that there is life after injury."

This is not political. I really do not care what your personal opinion is or has been on the politics of the war on terror. My primary objective is the soldiers, the 19-year-old kids who are standing watch on the wall. By going to battle, they have prevented the fray from coming to our soil.

These young men and women are my concern. I cannot tell you the number of times that I have seen battle-weary service personnel on the other side of the globe remove helmets, look at me through bleary eyes and say, "Mr. Roever, you spoke at my school. What are you doing here?"

I served eight months in the jungles of Vietnam. No one went there to visit or to encourage us service personnel. Not Bob Hope, not the Dallas Cowboy Cheerleaders (I would have remembered that!). Unfortunately, not even a chaplain.

So today, I go to our troops. Regardless of where they are— in the major hubs of Baghdad or on the most remote Forward Operating Base. I have gone to places in the Middle East that you would not believe and have gone to locations that not even my wife knows about. All I can say is, my guardian angels have worked overtime, lots of times!

Some have asked, "You'd do it all again, wouldn't you?" Then they mention some opportunity I have had in my career, such as speaking to presidents, addressing SHAPE (Supreme Headquarters Allied Powers Europe), or speaking at NATO (North Atlantic Treaty Organization).

"You'd do it all again, wouldn't you?"

"Do what?" I ask.

"You know…go to Vietnam…get blown up and all…"

I am no hero. I *did not* want to go to Vietnam in the first place. That was why I joined the Navy so I would not be drafted into the Army, which meant automatic deployment to Vietnam. I did not want to do *this* the first time. Why would I want to do *it* again?

Then one day in Baghdad, I held a dying young hero in my arms. He had been critically burned when a roadside bomb hit the fuel truck that he was driving.

As I held his charred body, I whispered words of comfort into a hole where an ear had been and watched as the last fleeting breath escaped his lips. I whispered softly, "You are more than a soldier. You are a sacrifice on the altar of freedom. On behalf of a grateful nation, I have come to say *thank you!*" The words had barely passed my lips when his body shuttered slightly and he slipped from my arms into the arms of God.

That day *it* was worth it for me. I knew that the only reason I was allowed to be in the war zone was because *it* had happened to me. That day, all the pain and disfigurement I have carried for the last forty-plus years was worth it.

Yes, it was an honor to speak with presidents and to address world powers. But to be able to bring hope and to foster courage in the lives of generations of young people is where I find my greatest fulfillment. To be the right man, at the right time, in the right place, with the right message of hope for a dying young hero made all that I have endured worthwhile.

Regardless of where you find yourself, I challenge you, as I have been challenged: "...Start running—and never quit! ...Keep your eyes on Jesus, who both began and finished this race we're in. Study how He did it. Because He never lost sight of where He was headed—that exhilarating finish in and with God—He could put up with anything along the way: Cross, shame, whatever. And now He's there, in the place of honor, right alongside God. When you find yourselves flagging in your faith, go over that story again, item by item, that long litany of hostility He plowed through. That will shoot adrenaline into your souls!"[1]

Although I find it difficult within myself to utter the words, "I'd do *it* again," I can truthfully say that I believe my doing *it* the first time has made a difference in lots of lives. Over the last several decades, it has meant the difference between eternal death and eternal life for untold numbers of young people throughout the world. And that, my friend, is sweet music to my soul.

[1] Hebrews 12:1-3 *The Message*

★   ★   ★

Chapter Three

Not At This Door

THE SPRING POPPED AND TWANGED AS IT RUBBED against the wooden frame on the screen door of the Quonset hut. Day-after-day, night-after-night, each time the door opened, the spring repeated the same irritating noises. It was the night openings that caused hearts to pound and throats to go dry for those who occupied the not-so-modern accommodations. Built for temporary housing, this Quonset hut had become a permanent fixture at Fort Sam Houston in San Antonio, Texas.

31

Long and narrow, the easily constructed Quonset hut was a building commonly used for military housing and administrative offices during World War II. Often seen in movies depicting that era, the building's floor plan was simple. A hallway ran down the center of the building with private rooms on either side. At the end of the hall, a single bathroom serviced all the occupants.

The main entrance to this particular Quonset hut was a solid-core, wooden door with a doorknob that wobbled uselessly in a worn-out hole in the doorframe. Coupled with it was the screen door and its popping, twanging spring. The well-worn wooden planks of the floor creaked and groaned under every footstep.

While this hut was not on some isolated island in the far-away Pacific, it was, however, very isolated, and very far away...

Brooke Army Medical Center, Fort Sam Houston Army Post, San Antonio, Texas.

Tucked away just beneath the hospital's east-side elevation, the isolation of the hut added to the perception that it and its occupants were of little importance.

Temporarily inhabiting the hut were the families of patients in the world's premier burn hospital—families who lived day-to-day, hour-to-hour, in suspense and fear. Their worst nightmares had become realities with their loved ones now as incarcerated as they were incinerated, lying in unspeakable pain and uncertainty.

No patient in Brooke Army Medical Center was there for convenience or by choice. Only the worst of burn victims were taken there. The isolation of the burn ward's Intensive Care Unit was matched only by the isolation felt by the families who occupied the hut next door. So close, yet far, far, away from the ones they loved. Separated by a world of pain—yet connected deeply in heart and spirit.

People died in BAMC. It was not a place of great expectations. I could be wrong, but I think the majority of the war injured who were admitted to the hospital died. On my ward, I certainly think that was the case.

It seemed that death came most often at night. In the lonely dark hours of early mornings, burn victims died alone. And when they died, the suffering was transferred from patient to family. The end of one drama in human suffering was the beginning of another.

In those same wee hours of the mornings, the screen door of the hut would open, its twanging, popping spring announcing the arrival of the Death Angel bearing tragic news of the passing of a husband ... a brother ... a son ... a dad.

Groaning floorboards warned of the approaching XO (Executive Officer on duty), a chaplain, and the attending physician whose synchronized steps were set in time to military tradition. Marching, marching, marching. The jarring of those steps on the wooden floor reverberated into every room of the hut. Like an executioner choosing his next victim, the Trio-of-Tragedy would soon stop and knock at the door of a family destined to receive unthinkable news.

Panicked by the sound of the footsteps, bodies tensed, ears strained. Listening. Dreading. Hoping. Hoping the steps would fall short of or pass on beyond the threshold of *their* door. Terrorized families huddled together, fearing the worst.

Horrified relief contradicted sanity when tears of joy in one chamber were discredited by muffled cries of denial in another.

Deep, guttural cries escaping from a twisted face burrowed into the shoulder of a chaplain in one room resonated throughout the building, clawing at the soul of every other occupant of the hut.

People credit me for my strength to survive the grenade explosion in Vietnam. I never feel at peace with that, and, as often as possible, as my friends and associates will attest, I pass the credit on to those who paid as dear a price as I ever did. None paid more dearly than my exceptionally lovely wife, who occupied the room just one door down from the hut's offensive screen door.

The human drama that played out in those early morning hours was not lost on her. The foreboding aroused by the opening of the hut's screen door would send the barely-twenty-year-old flying out of her bed onto her knees. Knowing her only help was in God, "in her distress she called to the LORD; she cried to her God for help. ...He heard her voice; her cry came before Him, into His ears."[1]

Facing the door in her small quarters in the ancient Quonset hut, her hands twined together in prayer, Brenda quietly hissed her hope-driven words to the Angel of Death, "Not at this door; not at this door!"

The long, lonely night was just beginning, and my heart was pounding in my chest as I lay on the small, hard bed. I was sweating profusely even though the air conditioner was purring out a steady rhythm. My tossing and turning had pulled the thinning, yellowed sheet from the corners of the military style bunk. My mind was flooded with the events of the day, and my racing imagination was hard to control. The "what-ifs" were circling like vultures over dead prey.

I did not want to be there.

The stark room where I spent countless lonely hours was plain with dirty white walls, its only furnishings a dresser and a bed. There were no pictures, no mirrors to reflect happier days, nothing to convey the warm, comfortable feelings of home. The room was simply lodging for transient souls in need of a place to lay tired bodies and troubled minds—souls who would stay there until ...

I did not want to be there.

The screen door moaned as it opened then slammed back against the doorframe like a clap of thunder in a summer storm. I heard the heels of the military boots on the wooden floor of the old barracks where my soul was hiding. Three pairs of boots marched simultaneously down the corridor. I rushed to my door, praying desperately that the footsteps were those of a family returning to their quarters. Knowing they were not.

"Please, Dear God, don't let them stop here!" My soul cried in anguish as hot tears coursed down my face. I slumped to the cold floor..."Not at my door tonight! Not at my door!"

I did not want to be there. I had not chosen this.

The scene would be repeated multiple times as the Death Angel hovered just out of sight. On several occasions I believe I saw his shadow, but he never stopped at my door.

My husband lived while many young Americans died. Their loving spouses would never feel the thrill of their husbands' touches again. These young men wanted to live as much as my husband did. They wanted to feel the ocean breezes on their faces and smell the fragrance of honeysuckle on the vine. They

*wanted to taste mom's apple pie and hear umpires
yell, "Play ball!" They wanted to know the thrill of
grandchildren bouncing on their knees.*

*Instead, they paid the ultimate price for freedom.
Their voices will never be heard again.*

Brenda's unwavering relationship with God and the strength
drawn from the words of the Bible, "The LORD is my strength
and my shield; My heart trusted in Him, and I am helped..."[2]
carried us both through the toughest times of our lives. Our
constant theme was, and still is, " I trust in you, O Lord; I say,
'You are my God.'"[3]

God gave us hope when there seemed no reason to hope.
He gave us strength when it seemed there was none left in us.
He gave us "**beauty** for **ashes**, the oil of joy for mourning, the
garment of praise for the spirit of heaviness; that we might be
called trees of righteousness, the planting of the LORD, **that He
might be glorified**."[4]

[1] Psalms 18:6 *Today's New International Version* (paraphrased)
[2] Psalms 28:7 *New King James Version*
[3] Psalms 31:14 *New King James Version*
[4] Isaiah 61:3 *New King James Version*

★ ★ ★

Chapter Four

A Merry Heart

I NEVER SHOULD HAVE SURVIVED when the grenade I was holding was hit by a sniper's bullet.

My face was gone, along with my right ear, my hair, my nose, my lips, my right eyelid, as well as nearly half the skin from my entire body. My thumb and fingers were hanging by tendons. My chest was blown open exposing my heart, yet I continued to breathe. I had escaped with my life.

More than 40 years have passed since that day of living hell. It is impossible to forget. Every morning when I stick on my spare parts and see the scars that cover my body and, worse yet, when I see my face, I am reminded of that fateful day. I often say that it would not be so bad if all the scars were beneath my clothing, but that is not the way life happened for me. The devastation is right out there for all to see.

Being scarred and disfigured does, however, have its interesting moments. Children who see me sometimes cry, turn away, and run into stuff.

Do not feel sorry for me. I have long since learned to turn my misery into ministry, my disability into ability, my tragedy into triumph.

Learning all this started when I met Paul in the hospital that was my cocoon, my hiding place, for a year and two months following my injury.

Paul had been piloting a small crop-duster plane when a wing fell off and the plane crashed and burst into flames. He had no ears, no nose, no lips. He was a mess. Although he was burned over more than 50 percent of his body, he, too, miraculously survived.

Because we shared the torment of facial burns, we became best friends. In fact, it was Paul who taught me the virtues of growling, spitting, and convulsing spasmodically.

As we traversed the hospital, we became known as the *Crispy Critters.*

We did everything together. We switched the signs, MEN and WOMEN, on restroom doors. We hid non-ambulatory patients' wheelchairs from them. You know, just boys being boys.

One thing you should understand about burns. They hurt! The burns themselves are excruciating, but added to that is the pain of skin grafts. Skin is stripped from where the body is not burned and put onto places where it is burned. The harvest sites hurt just as badly as the burn sites. Burn survivors want to shout to the world, "Don't touch me—anywhere!"

Paul and I were really a sight to behold. We wore matching pajama bottoms and blue robes draped over our shoulders to cause as little friction to our upper extremities as possible. Paul had no features at all. I, at least, had one ear and half my face. Both of us suffered from scarred skin that had contracted, drawing our arms and chins to our chests.

We could barely walk, and most of the time our paths could be traced by the smears of blood we left on the floors of the hospital. We did not care what we looked like. We were both grateful just to be alive.

One day we left our ward to get some exercise, which consisted of nothing more than our shuffling cautiously down the hospital hallways. Since it was almost noon, we rode the freight elevator down to the basement to have lunch in the cafeteria. After we finished eating that day, one of our greatest adventures began.

It was time to return to our ward, but, to our dismay, the freight elevator had broken down. We would be forced to walk up several flights of stairs, which would be torture because of the recent skin harvests taken from our legs, or take the public elevator, which we hated doing because other people would be on the elevator with us.

We chose the elevator.

Since we were in the basement, we were the first to board, but when the elevator stopped at the first floor, an onslaught of passengers invaded the small space. This was not good news. We could not bear to be touched, so we backed as far as we could into opposite corners. The crowd began pressing against our bodies, unintentionally inflicting unimaginable pain.

Paul winked at me, which was really hard to do since he had no eyelid, and right on cue, we began convulsing, growling, and spitting (our version of foaming at the mouth). Sweet Revenge! We were now inflicting great emotional discomfort on the other passengers.

The elevator stopped immediately and all the people vacated. Thank God, the elevator had stopped at a floor level!

Our convulsions turned into laughter as people crawled all over each other in their mad dash to escape. We pushed the button, and just the two of us made the rest of the journey up to our ward.

To our amazement, when the elevator door opened, one of the medics who had exited with the crowd, had beaten us to our ward by running up the stairs.

After I finally was released from the hospital, one of my joys was to drive my car. I was stopped at a traffic light one day, and I watched a guy who was staring at me drive his car right into a Dairy Queen. Bam! — Right through the plate glass window. The window did have **Drive In** written on it. And he did. I was laughing my head off (what was left of it).

The traffic light where I was sitting kept changing colors, and the guy behind me was changing colors, too. It dawned on me that I had better go, or he might get out of his car and come after me.

I took off, only to realize I was running a red light. I hit my brakes, and the man behind me plowed into the rear of my car. I was laughing hysterically at the circumstances. Two wrecks in two minutes, all because of my face!

I laughed till I was crying. I got out of my car to apologize. Everyone at the Dairy Queen thought I was drunk. Then they saw me with my one eye, one ear, one nostril, no hair, and no face, and they thought they were drunk!

Little kids are so innocent in their questions about my disfigurement. Kids do not understand war, so I generally answer

43

their questions with, "Don't play with matches!" Most are satisfied with that answer, but a few can be rather obnoxious.

One daring five-year-old approached me with hands on hips, "What happened to your face?"

Evidently I did not respond quickly enough to satisfy his curiosity, so he screamed, "WHAT HAPPENED TO YOUR FACE!" His attitude was a bit more than I could tolerate.

Where it came from, I do not know. I simply replied, "Don't eat oatmeal!"

Immediately his hands covered his face, and he went screaming to his mother. How was I supposed to know that he had eaten oatmeal for breakfast? Last report I heard was that he has never eaten oatmeal again—bad news for the Quaker company.

Sometimes teenagers approach me in a different way. One guy boldly asked, "Hey, Dude, what happened to your face?"

My reply to this uncouth guy? "I was burned bobbing for French fries."

He must have been stoned. With a faraway look in his eyes, he said, "Whoa, Dude. Did you get one?"

My prosthetic ear used to be a plastic, stick-on apparatus. Now, I have the uptown, snap-on version. Occasionally, the old ear would fall off because of perspiration collecting under it.

Years ago, I was preaching in Jamaica on a hot, sticky night when suddenly the entire crowd began to suck air like a Hoover vacuum cleaner. As shock registered on their faces, I recoiled.

I feared the worst, thinking that my fly had broken, or some other such malady had occurred, but I soon realized they were staring at my shoulder.

My ear had fallen off while I was preaching and was perched precariously on my right shoulder.   In a panic, I reached to where my ear was lying face up (as if waiting to hear from God above), grabbed it, and stuck it back onto the side of my head.

How do you explain that to a crowd of people for whom Voodoo is not an oddity? "Sorry folks, my ear fell off. I'm just sticking it back on."

Spellbound, they did not make a move. They did not even blink until someone yelled, "It's a miracle, mon! There IS a GOD!"   It turned out to be a great meeting, and many people made decisions that night to follow Christ!

That is not the only "earie" experience in my life. I have the unprecedented privilege of working with the Department of Defense (DOD) in the Comprehensive Soldier Fitness program with the official title of Resiliency Coach. Those who most need encouragement are conversely those who are typically in the most dangerous places.

Late one night, or should I say early one morning, I was on a mission in Iraq with some Special Forces teams. Since I was a Brown Water Black Beret in Vietnam, I fit pretty comfortably with them.

During the Vietnam War, I was a simple Petty Officer, but for my role with the DOD and Central Command in the war on terror, I move about with the rank of O-7 (one-star general) only for protocol. With that rank, I have worldwide access to generals of great fame. Most Special Forces troops, however, set aside rank to insure harmonious team effort, so my O-7 did not mean fame with these Special Forces guys. So it just must have been the right tone of voice, that utterance of a growl that followed a bizarre event.

The body armor I wear while in a combat zone is identical to that of all other soldiers, and Kevlar is actually quite heavy, bringing the body-armor weight to about 70 pounds. As we were boarding a giant C-130 one night in Iraq, I was struggling to put on my body armor. I slipped my left arm through the vest, and while trying to throw the armor onto my right shoulder, the heavy plating hit my right artificial ear.

It was Jamaica all over again… My ear fell off.

It was pitch black and we were in a combat operational zone, so no one dared turn on a flashlight for any reason. C-130 ramps have many channels, rollers, and divots—a plethora of places for an ear to cunningly hide itself.

Now, back to that growl. Some kind of authority passed my lips as I shouted, "My ear fell off. Find it!"

Do you know what it looks like to see America's finest, biggest, baddest, enemy-terrifying, special-operations teams down on their knees on the ramp of a C-130 in the middle of the night in Iraq, feeling around for a plastic ear?

I started laughing. I could not help myself. One of them yelled, "Why are you laughing? You didn't lose your ear. You're just messing with us!"

"No, honestly," I replied, "my ear did fall off, and one of you is really close to it because I can hear you breathing!"

The joke was on me when one of them asked, "Dude, is it me?"

We did find the ear, and I have all my pieces back. I guess you can say I had to pull myself together again.

★   ★   ★

If you have not figured it out yet, I am trying to tell you that a merry heart is good medicine. The wisest man who ever lived said it this way, "A cheerful disposition is good for your health."[1]

At the polar opposite, depression drains one's strength. "Gloom and doom leave you bone-tired."

I have learned those lessons well, and I want you to understand the triumph that the Lord has brought out of the tragedies in my life.

When things go wrong for us, we have two choices. We can sit down and cry, saying, "Poor me," and bury our faces in the sand and never accomplish anything. Of course, you know what is exposed when one's head is buried in the sand!

Just as a sidebar: Many will agree with the popular philosophy of today that says a particular situation was brought about because of genetics or, perhaps, the environment. After all, according to political correctness, we really are not responsible, and there is no such thing as right or wrong. No grade is failing.

Society would justify one such as I sitting on a bar stool, popping tops and sucking suds. One doctor said to me when I was being released after fourteen months of hospitalization, "Take your veteran's allotment for land, buy a farm in the Ohio Valley, and let your wife go to town. Save yourself the embarrassment of being in public."

The second choice we have in times of difficulty is to commit the situation into the hands of God and rejoice.

How can we possibly rejoice when everything seems to be falling apart? First we need to understand that whatever happens in our lives has not taken God by surprise, and if He is not surprised, then He knows the way for us to get through it. And I do not mean just barely scraping by; I mean triumphing.

Second, "We are assured and know that God being a partner in their labor, all things work together **and are fitting into a plan**

48

for good...for those who love God and are called according to His design and purpose." [2]

Did you get that? **All things—not part of or some of—all things work together for good.** We always want to make exceptions: "But in this situation..." "But you just don't understand..." "But that just cannot be what God meant in my circumstances..."

In this, like in every other situation, we always have a choice. We can submit to God, rejoice in Him, and let Him bring triumph out of our difficulties, or we can go on wallowing in our miseries and feeling sorry for ourselves. Frankly, I do not want to live with that second choice.

I am not saying that my life has been easy and that there have not been times of great despair. What I am saying is this. Wherever my path has taken me, God has walked by my side. His promise *to all of us* is that He will never leave us or forsake us. "...For He [God] Himself has said, I will not in any way fail you nor give you up nor leave you without support. I will not, I will not, I will not in any degree leave you helpless nor forsake nor let you down, nor relax My hold on you! Assuredly not!" [3]

Notice how He repeats, "I will not" three times? He wants us to get it. He is *never* going to leave us on our own!

If I had taken the advice of the doctors and the psychologists, I would have shriveled up within myself, propped my feet up on the coffee table, and spent my life watching soap operas.

But *no!* I chose to follow a dream and placed this scarred

face and crippled body on the frontlines—in high schools, on military installations, on television, and in travels around the world, sharing the Good News of Jesus Christ and His saving and restoring power.

I am glad the Lord trusted me with my scars.

Has it been easy? Absolutely not, but I have learned some powerful lessons along the way. I do know this: "I have strength for all things in Christ Who empowers me. I am ready for anything and equal to anything through Him Who infuses inner strength into me; I am self-sufficient in Christ's sufficiency." [4]

He will mold each of us, using what we are and what happens to us to make a difference in this world.

What has He entrusted to you? Do not rebel against Him. All things—not part of, or some of—but all things will work together for good to those who love Him and are called according to His purpose.

I have laughed my way out of hell, and I am going to laugh my way through Heaven's pearly gates because the joy of the Lord is (my) strength! [5]

[1] Proverbs 17:22 The Message Bible
[2] Romans 8:28 Amplified Bible
[3] Hebrews 13:5 Amplified Bible
[4] Philippians 4:13 Amplified Bible
[5] Nehemiah 8:10 Amplified Bible

★   ★   ★

Chapter Five

Worth Living For

CALLED HANDSHAKE ENGINES, they are nothing more than little Briggs and Stratton lawnmower motors with long shafts connected to them and propellers fastened to the ends of the shafts. During the war, the United States government provided these engines for the Vietnamese people, and the motors with their distinct sound can still be found all over Vietnam. The people use them to propel their *sampans,* canoe-like boats, which are common modes of transport throughout Southeast Asia.

As we started westward on the Vam Co Tay River toward Cambodia, the sampans were whizzing past us in every direction. It had been many years since I was injured here, but the pain and the memories never go away.

The old water taxi I rented was about 50 feet long and 10 feet wide. During the war, I would board old boats like this searching for Viet Cong—with my heart pounding and my M16 cocked and ready, I would search through the jam-packed boats. Carefully studying identification documents of each of the scores of people onboard, I looked for any discrepancy that would give me a clue as to illegal travelers, communists in disguise.

Now I was back on a river taxi. There were no disguises anywhere in the country this day. They were all communists. I was not scrutinizing identification documents; they were scrutinizing mine.

Having paid the boat captain 400 U.S. dollars, which amounted to about two years' salary in Vietnam, the captain gladly gave me the entire boat—under his command, of course. My cameraman, the interpreter, my son, and I were its only passengers.

We were on a journey into the interior of Vietnam, a journey back to where my face was blown off. Fingers were blown off. My ear and hair were blown off.

People have asked me many times since, "Why would you do that to yourself? Why go back to where you were injured?"

Laughing, I tell them I went back to look for my ear, that I wanted to find my thumb, and that maybe, just maybe, over by a tree I would find my eyelid and nose.

In reality, I was looking for my heart. I wanted to see what my feelings would be when put to the ultimate test of being there and remembering. Would I be filled with love for that which I had sacrificed? Would I be filled with hatred because of the immense price I had paid?

The captain beached the boat at the exact place where I was injured. I easily recognized the location by the bend in the river that was burned indelibly in my memory.

It had taken us a full day of traveling the jungle waterways to get back to the village where so much pain began for me. Before starting the trip, I had been told that I would be the first American to go back into that part of Vietnam since 1975.

What would happen when the people saw me?

What did happen changed my life forever.

Just as we beached the boat, an old man stepped out of the tree line onto a worn path that led down to the riverbank. Our arrival surprised him, but his surprise had only just begun. My son, Matthew, looked just like I did during the war. His jaw has the familiar jut, his eyes the same shape and piercing blue color, his shoulders as broad as my own.

The old man looked at my son like he was seeing a ghost. Then he looked at me. A frenzy of words in Vietnamese poured out of him as he talked to my interpreter.

The interpreter looked at me, and with the same frenzy, exclaimed, "This old man says he knows you!"

Incredulously, I said, "He doesn't know me. It's been too many years."

"No, Mr. Dave, he does know you. He says you are *Mop Det.*"

"*Mop Det?*" That was the nickname the children of the village had given me.

"Yes, Mr. Dave, he knows you. He thought you were dead! He saw you on fire, burning here, and he saw the helicopter come pick you up. He said every year they tell the children about *Mop Det* who died fighting for them. He says he is so happy you are not dead!"

I looked at my son as tears rolled down my face. Matt asked, "Dad, are you all right? Don't lose it now, and leave me in this jungle with no way back."

"I'm fine, Matt. I'm just overwhelmed that they remember. They remember the sacrifice and celebrate it every year.

"The fact that these people remember takes years of pain away. Because they remember, it is all worth it."

Suddenly, like a divine revelation, I understood something I had never understood about Christ.

"Because this village remembers me, because they remember

the sacrifice, my pain is no longer meaningless." It meant so much to me that they still remembered my sacrifice.

One day, Christ will come back and put His feet down on the bank of my river, and I will look at Him and say, "I remember You. And I've told my children about You, and we have remembered Your sacrifice."

He will say, "You've made My heart rejoice because you cared enough to remember My sacrifice. You have understood the significance of My pain."

I did not die for my country or for Vietnam, as those precious people in the village had thought, but I am prepared to die for what I believe in.

People ask me, "Is there *anything* worth dying for?"

If there is nothing worth dying for, and nothing greater or higher than myself worth sacrificing for, then the question is no longer, "Is there anything worth dying for?" The question is, "Is there anything worth living for?"

With everything in me, I believe there is something worth living for. Therefore, there is something worth dying for. The Apostle Paul said it so well in his letter to the church in Philippi. "Whatever were gains to me I now consider loss for the sake of Christ. What is more, I consider everything a loss because of the **surpassing worth of knowing Christ Jesus my Lord,** for whose sake I have lost all things. I consider them garbage that I may gain Christ and be found in Him...I want to know Christ—yes, to know the power of His resurrection and participation in His sufferings, becoming like Him…"[1]

So I will sacrifice my life by living for the young people of this nation, giving everything I have for this cause, so that the next generation may know Christ the way I know Him. That while they are still young, before they are maimed and scarred and wasted by sin, I can interrupt their slide to destruction by giving them something worth living for!

I am with the Apostle Paul in this all the way. He continues in his letter to the Philippians, "I'm not saying that I have this all together, that I have it made. But I am well on my way, reaching out for Christ, Who has so wondrously reached out for me. Friends, don't get me wrong: By no means do I count myself an expert in all of this, but **I've got my eye on the goal**, where God is beckoning us onward—to Jesus. **I'm off and running, and I'm not turning back.**"[2]

Is there something worth living for? Oh, yeah.

Is there something worth dying for? You better believe it.

His Name is Jesus!!

[1] Philippians 3:7-10 *Today's New International Version*
[2] Philippians 3:12-13 *The Message*

★   ★   ★

Chapter Six

Forgiving Love

A BABY BOOMER—I AM ONE. I am part of *that* generation. We were also flower children. I do not know if that means we were blooming idiots or just a growth on somebody's shelf. We were and are a generation that changed the destiny of a nation.

I am in somewhat of a reflective mood as I write, remembering how God has saved me from death, saved me from sin, and saved me from myself. Sometimes I think I am my own worst enemy. In reality, that is true of all of us.

From the mid 70's through the 80's, while my children were growing up, so was their dad. After my injury in Vietnam, I had to start all over. I was trying to find myself. During those years, my wife and children endured some of the hardest days a family could know.

Telling you this requires two things of you. One, that you understand that this is not easy. Two, that you understand that you are not alone in your suffering. You will find comfort in these words because other people have faced some of the same fears and anxieties of life that you are facing, and, having conquered them, they have immerged on the other side as better people.

In public, I learned to make people laugh, but in private, I could only remember how to cry. I would sit in front of a mirror, looking at myself with immense hatred and rejection. I despised my scars and abhorred everything I saw. I would berate myself with immeasurable disdain while my wife would weep and try to comfort me.

I would push her away saying, "Baby, you can't understand. *That* is not me anymore. That *thing* in the mirror is not me! I want my face back. I want my fingers back. *I want my life back!*"

There were times when I would load a pistol, hold it to my head, and beg God to please kill me before I killed myself. All of my life I had been taught to believe that if I killed myself, I would go to hell. I felt that if somehow I could talk God into killing me, I would go to Heaven.

I wanted somebody to do something, and do it quickly. I just could not take it anymore. What I did not know was that somebody was doing something.

My young daughter was standing outside my bedroom door during these episodes. She heard me reject her mother's pleas. She heard me curse myself. In terror she would run to her room, crawl up onto her bed, and pray, "Jesus, please help Daddy not to hurt himself!"

The words and actions that I assumed were hidden behind closed doors were being laid at the gates of Heaven through the prayers of a child. The Bible says to "…pray for each other so that you may be healed. The prayer of a righteous person (a child in this case) is powerful and effective."[1]

In 1993, I traveled back to Vietnam. I went back to the bank of the river where in 1969 my face was ripped from me by a hand grenade explosion, where fingers were left dangling by tendons, where my chest was ripped open, and I could see my heart beating, where nearly half of my skin and 60 pounds of flesh were blown off my body.

When I returned to the site of my injury, I was trying to close the gap in the vicious cycle my life had been on for 25 years. How could this have happened to me? How did I survive? Just being there brought healing.

I returned home from that trip, and my daughter, who was a teenager by that time, met me with a song that she had written.

The song spoke of a little girl standing by her momma and daddy's door "hearing things that she could not ignore." The song went on to say it was a forgiving love and a forgiving grace, "the kind that held my momma's and daddy's love firmly fixed in place."

As she sang to me, I realized that all the things I thought were so cleverly hidden had been exposed to my family.

It would be terribly wrong of me not to tell why I do not think of suicide any more and do not continually curse and berate myself. It is the same reason I have filled so many pulpits, spoken in so many schools, and traveled all over the world speaking to the military.

It is not because I am a good man. It is simply because God answered the prayers of my beloved wife. God answered the prayers of my precious daughter.

I realize that God spared me from certain death in Vietnam, and He spared me from self-destruction through the loving support of my family and friends.

Sometimes I fear that an unrealistic image has been cast of me as a man who sailed through personal injury and disfigurement without marital stress and without deep scarring of the soul. The truth is, my spirit was battered and my marriage suffered greatly, but God... God intervened! God gave me tremendous victory. Out of my chaos, peace was restored.

Perhaps now, you can understand my passion for reaching

out to our young wounded warriors. If God can take this beat-up, burned-up piece of clay and restore me, He can do the same in their lives, too.

Just for the record, you do not have to be blown-up in Vietnam or injured in Iraq or Afghanistan to be a wounded warrior. Some of you live with great physical pain every day. Some of you have had your very hearts ripped from you by the loss of love either through death, divorce, or infidelity. Some of you are haunted with memories of the past. Many of you have experienced such emotional trauma that it seems it would be easier to quit than to go on.

Let me remind you that Jesus endured the stripes on His back for your healing. How do I know that God will help you? He came to me, and I am a living example that God intervenes in man's affairs.

With everything in me, I believe I have endured what I have so that I can say to you today, "…the Lord has anointed and qualified me to preach the Gospel of good tidings to the meek, the poor, and afflicted; …to proclaim liberty to the [physical and spiritual] captives and the opening of the prison and of the eyes to those who are bound…" [2]

God came to me in my darkest hour, and He delivered me from myself.

Trust Him. There is immeasurable hope for you that only He can give. "For I know the plans I have for you," declares the

LORD, "plans to prosper you and not to harm you, plans to give you hope and a future." [3]

[1] James 5:16 *Today's New International Version*
[2] Isaiah 61:1 *Amplified Bible*
[3] Jeremiah 29:11 *Today's New International Version*

★   ★   ★

Chapter Seven

Inches and Seconds

T HE HELICOPTER LANDED, BLOWING DUST SKY-HIGH. All of us scrambled to get off the chopper, dragging our *battle rattle* (personal body armor) with us as we moved toward the concrete barriers of the FOB (Forward Operating Base) at Kirkuk, Iraq. Sometimes called T-walls, these concrete barriers are about 15 feet tall and serve as temporary walls to protect the FOB from insurgents. They also limit the damage from incoming mortar rounds and rocket fire.

The commanding officer of the FOB, an exuberant colonel, was so excited about my arrival that he made me feel like I was the lone friend of his troops. Just inches from my face, a cameraman from the *Discovery TV Network* was filming the meeting. The film crew seemed infatuated by the fact that a Vietnam veteran was showing up in an Iraqi war.

How can wars that are worlds and decades apart have a common denominator? Well, believe me, they do. To the soldier, it is not where he fights or even for whom he is fighting. The common denominator is the cause—the cause of freedom. Vietnam, Iraq, Somalia, Kosovo, the list goes on and on of places where American soldiers have bled and died for freedom.

The key word there is *American* soldiers. Americans have fought at different times and in different theaters but share the common belief that liberty and freedom are fundamental basics to the human achievement of happiness.

As I walked toward the center of the FOB, hundreds of troops were already waiting for us. The commanding general and the FOB colonel led the way; the television crew followed; an over-the-hill Vietnam Vet held the middle ground. It was quite a procession.

With only a few moments left before I was to address this august body of young heroes, the colonel began telling me of the unfortunate and untimely death of his interpreter, an American of Middle Eastern descent.

"The two of us were standing there talking when I heard the sickening sound of a bullet hitting him. He dropped to the ground and died, Mr. Roever."

The colonel continued, "I was only inches from him. In a few seconds, I would have been standing exactly where he was!

"Do you understand me, Mr. Roever? This is a war of inches and seconds ... inches and seconds." His eyes bored into my own.

Then he looked away and repeated a third time, "...*inches and seconds.*"

Often we fail to understand how extremely important inches and seconds are in our lives. An architect or an engineer knows how critical an inch is. A good comedian knows how critical timing is. A good soldier knows how critical an inch, as well as a second, is. In comedy, timing can mean success or failure. In war, it can mean life or death.

For me, both inches and seconds were critical that fateful day in Vietnam when I pulled back to throw a white phosphorous grenade. It was about six inches from my head. Had it been four inches or eight inches, the sniper's bullet, in all likelihood, would not have hit it. Had the grenade left my hand just a second earlier, the bullet would have missed it, and the damage would have been done to the enemy rather than to me. From another perspective, because the sniper's aim was off about six inches, the bullet hit the grenade instead of my head. In that case, six inches was the difference between my living and dying that day.

In life, the consequences are eternal. We are told to "be wise as serpents"[1] as we go through this life.

Now why would Jesus say that?

Well, I have learned a thing or two about snakes. Snakes are pros at escaping. Their first line of defense is to stay out of harm's way, and to do this, they have to be constantly alert to dangers.

It is critical that we, too, be constantly alert...always aware of what is going on around us so that we are not caught in one of the traps that the enemy of our souls sets for us. Satan is singularly focused: he "comes only to steal and kill and destroy."[2]

Be sharp. Be alert. Do not mess around where you know there is danger. Be wise as a serpent; put on your track shoes and run for your life.

You know what I am talking about. If somebody offers you drugs or "a good time," or whatever—stuff that you know will not be good for you, the split-second decision you make can mean the difference between destroying your life and saving it.

This book may be landing in your hands at a moment of crucial timing in your life. I want you to understand something. There is a way out. "Don't be afraid, I've redeemed you. I've called your name. You're mine. When you're in over your head, I'll be there with you. When you're in rough waters, you will not go down. When you're between a rock and a hard place, it won't be a dead end— Because I am God, your personal God..." [3]

Sometimes, all we have are inches and seconds in which to make decisions that will shape the rest of our lives. Decide wisely and leave the results in God's hands.

An excellent interpreter for the military was lost on the battlefield in Iraq that day, but the lessons learned from his demise may well be the secret of success for those who are quick to learn.

[1] Matthew 10:16 *New King James Version*
[2] John 10:10 *Today's New International Version*
[3] Isaiah 43:1-3 *The Message*

★   ★   ★

Chapter Eight

Crackers in my Bed

BEADS OF WATER SKEWED HIS SHARP EYE as he took focus, aimed and fired. It is hard to shoot an anti-tank, B-40 rocket at a bobbing fiberglass boat. Stuff gets in the way.

For who knows how long, the Viet Cong had waited patiently, anticipating the opportune moment to take our lives.

It was a warm relaxing evening, and I was sitting in the coxswain's chair with my feet propped up on the instrument panel as the engines idled. Nothing out of the ordinary was happening, so I sat quietly, listening to the rain spill from the canopy and splash onto the deck of the PBR (River Patrol Boat). I had been in Vietnam for over six months without so much as a scratch, and I was thinking, "I might just get through this alive."

The rain started falling harder on that seemingly God-forsaken river, the Vam Co Tay. My feet were so high on the instrument panel that I could see through my toes. I was feeling a bit sleepy, but sleep never came easily. There was always that little edge, like trying to walk with a pebble in your shoe while concentrating on the mountain you must climb, or like lying on clean sheets and feeling the crumbs from the crackers you have been eating rub against your skin. I knew I was not going to sleep. I was just drowsy enough for it to be bothersome. And bothered I was!

For whatever reason, I dropped my feet to the deck, and in one fluid motion, sprang up, grabbed the twin throttles that would release diesel fuel into the two giant engines that were incased near the center of the boat.

The cracker crumbs in my bed or the pebble in my shoe... something, or **Someone**, had made me very uncomfortable. A horrific uneasiness pressed me into responding as if we were under attack. I firewalled the throttles.

Both V-6 Detroit diesel engines leaped into immediate full-power thrust against the Jacuzzi jets as the boat responded with unbelievably quick acceleration. Aboard this state-of-the-art navy vessel with me were a mid-ship gunner who stood between two M60 machine guns, a forward gunner with twin .50 caliber machine guns, and the aft gunner who manned a .50 caliber machine gun and a Mark18 grenade launcher.

Not expecting the jolt created by the powerful thrust of the jets as I slammed the throttles forward, the other three guys were grabbing for anything to keep from falling or being impaled on the surrounding equipment.

Only seconds later, a huge explosion blew—not on our boat, not in the water—but in the foliage that had completely camouflaged the enemy. Locating the explosion was easy. A plume of black smoke rose from behind the stump of a tree. We opened fire, then reversed our course and made another firing run, only to realize we were not receiving enemy fire.

We waited, holding the enemy's location in our crosshairs, adrenaline flowing full-bore, hearts pounding out of our chests.

From the tree line, uniformed members of the Army of the Republic of Vietnam (ARVN—*friendlies*) emerged. They were laughing and indicating for us to stop all action.

As they approached, we held them carefully at gunpoint until we were satisfied that they were *friendlies*. One of them who spoke English fluently explained to us, as Paul Harvey would say, "the rest of the story."

While we had been drifting quietly, though uneasily, down

the river in a somewhat relaxed state—feet on the instrument panel, leaning against the turrets, daydreaming of sweethearts back home—the Viet Cong were setting an ambush for us.

One of the Viet Cong had crouched down to a squatting position with a B-40, anti-tank, rocket-propelled grenade focused on our boat. The difficulty of aiming in the pouring rain was making it hard enough to stay on target, but then a crazy coxswain with *crackers in his bed* leaped to his feet for no apparent reason and firewalled the throttles, causing the boat to leap into action.

The enemy, desperately wanting to destroy our heavily armed boat, and us along with it, swung his rocket launcher, tracing the boat's exit, and squeezed the trigger just as his weapon aligned with a tree in front of him. The rocket exploded, killing him and his comrades.

Do I believe for a minute that I acted solely on a hunch? Not in a lifetime. There is not a shred of doubt in my mind. God was directing my actions that day.

It is so important for us to pay attention to the nudges, the unsettled feelings that something is "just not right."

The Apostle Peter gave us this caution. "Keep a cool head. Stay alert. The Devil is poised to pounce, and would like nothing better than to catch you napping. Keep your guard up..."[1]

We need to be keenly sensitive to God's nudging because the

enemy of our souls will set an ambush against us. The Bible teaches us to be instant, in season and out of season. That means we must respond without delay, whether it is convenient or inconvenient. When the Spirit within you says to move, it does not matter if you are sitting quietly in your recliner or if you are in a combat zone somewhere in the world, move!

When the Spirit urges you to pray, do not put it off. Someone's life may be at stake. There are many documented cases of lives that have been saved and injuries prevented because someone was willing to pay attention and respond to the nudging to pray.

In my own case, when the white phosphorus grenade blew up in my hand, it was the middle of the night where my parents lived on the other side of the world. At the exact moment of the explosion, my mother bolted upright in bed, awakened my dad, and said, "It's Davey! We need to pray!" I know I am alive today because they prayed.

Many nights, I am awakened, not by noise, or light, or vibrations, but by a gentle nudge of the Holy Spirit, and I begin to pray. God allows us to be uncomfortable in order to keep our edge against the enemy. Complacency can be catastrophic.

The enemy will set an ambush, but he cannot succeed against us when we are sensitive and obedient to God. "God is faithful to His Word and to His compassionate nature, and He can be trusted not to let you be tempted and tried and assayed beyond your ability and strength of resistance and power to endure, but with the temptation He will always also provide the way out, the means of escape to a landing place, that you may be capable and strong and powerful to bear up under it patiently."[2]

And, get this: we do not have to be the originator of the enemy's demise. The enemy will sometimes destroy himself! My obedience in firewalling those engines that day disoriented my enemy by disrupting his line of sight. When he reacted to my action of obedience, he destroyed himself.

"To obey is better than sacrifice."[3] My obedience that day, as foolish as it may have first appeared, prevented anyone on our boat from being sacrificed on the altar for freedom. I am not the hero in this story. God is. He turned a potential tragedy into a very real victory. When we let God arise, our enemies will scatter.[4]

During times of economic uncertainty, in every twist and turn of life, the enemy has carefully laid ambush to inflict havoc in the lives of the children of God. Now, more than ever, we need to fine-tune our sensitivity to the nudging of the Holy Spirit.

I do not say this to scare you. We never need to live in fear for God is with us. "Fear not, there is nothing to fear, for I (God) am with you; do not look around you in terror and be dismayed, for I am your God. I will strengthen and harden you to difficulties, yes, I will help you; yes, I will hold you up and retain you with My victorious right hand of rightness and justice."[5]

What a powerful promise from God Himself!

   As for me, I am committed to staying alert at all times and committed to responding quickly at the slightest nudging of the Spirit of God. I will only relax as much as the *crackers in my bed* will allow me!

[1] I Peter 5:8-9 *The Message Bible*
[2] I Corinthians 10:13 *The Amplified Bible*
[3] I Samuel 15:22 *King James Bible*
[4] Psalm 68:1 *King James Bible (paraphrased)*
[5] Isaiah 41:10 *The Amplified Bible*

Chapter Nine

11:59 p.m.

WHEN I TOUR WITH THE MILITARY, I am classified as a D.V., a Distinguished Visitor. With the Air Force, I am designated an **0-7**, which is the same as a one-star general. It would be great to be paid for that rank, but my O-7 is only for protocol. The designation allows me to work with the generals in the field and gives me access to thousands of troops; it virtually grants me unrestricted travel in military zones.

Flying from Kuwait one night in a private jet used by a leading general in the war on terror, we landed in Baghdad and pulled up alongside a gigantic C-130 cargo plane used to transport troops and tons of equipment into the battlefields of Iraq and Afghanistan.

Normally, C-130s are loaded with trucks, armaments, food supplies, and all things necessary for our troops. I suspect even a tank could fit into its cargo bay. What was about to be taken aboard the giant aircraft that night, however, was the most priceless "cargo" I have ever seen a C-130 carry.

It was 11:59 p.m. in Baghdad as we deplaned, and I watched a truck back up to the C-130. Two rows of soldiers stood at smart attention on either side of the loading ramp. Immediately, I knew what was happening. This was a patriot service.

In all actuality, I could have picked up the cargo by myself and carried it in my arms. The cargo was a fallen hero, a great young American who had given his life on Thanksgiving morning.

In the oppressive darkness of Baghdad at midnight, the remains of a young warrior were loaded onto the C-130 as the only "cargo" destined for the United States. During this unspeakable moment of honor and loss, I choked back tears.

The chaplain who would conduct this intensely hallowed occasion recognized me as I stood outside the aircraft. He invited me in. I felt completely out of my element. I had not been there when this hero was killed, and, at the moment, I did not even know with what unit he had served.

I had just arrived in country and had not yet begun my itinerary that would extend into the following month, leaving me exhausted. Here at the very beginning of my commitment to the troops, this emotional hit staggered me. I stood with the chaplain behind the remains of this hero, and as the brilliant *Red, White and Blue* was draped over his casket, the chaplain asked me to pray.

I prayed for his mother and father; I prayed for the soldiers who stood there with blood, mud, and spent gunpowder on their faces; and I prayed for this young fallen hero's very best friend. That friend back home who might not get all the information about this tragic event — the kid he grew up with. Not just a friend, but his **very best friend**. I prayed that God would send someone to comfort his very best friend.

The engine of a Black Hawk whined as it spooled up, turning the giant blades that swished through the thick, suffocating Baghdad night air. When I finished praying and opened my eyes, I saw my general friend tap his watch and circle his finger in the air, signaling for me to wrap it up, that we had to go.

• • •

I did seventy missions on that trip. It totally exhausted me, physically, mentally, and emotionally. I am no young buck anymore. While my heart empathizes with the soldiers who serve a year or more on each deployment, and many serve multiple deployments, sometimes three, four and even five deployments, I do not compare myself to them, but I was exhausted.

My return home brought me through the giant Hartsfield-Jackson International Airport in Atlanta. Everything goes through Atlanta. When Jesus returns, and we start our journey to Heaven, I am sure we are all going to have to go through Atlanta and get another boarding pass.

Waiting at the gate where my flight was to depart for Colorado Springs, I read the sign that said the plane was scheduled to depart at 11:59 p.m. How ridiculous! 11:59 p.m. Why not just say midnight? Do not give me this 11:59 p.m. stuff. It was a midnight departure, and I chose to inform the agent at the gate that this plane would not leave at 11:59 p.m. She laughed because it was such a ludicrous thought, and who really cared?

But something was happening in my spirit. I was actually wondering, *What is missing?* The departure time should have been rounded-up to 12:00 midnight, but because it was posted as 11:59 p.m., it reminded me of "leaving the ninety-nine for the one." The Bible talks about a shepherd who had a hundred sheep, but one went missing: so he left the ninety-nine to go search for the one that was lost. He could not rest until he had found that one.[1]

Are you tracking with me? Do you understand where I am going with this? That night in the Atlanta airport, something felt very unfinished.

A few moments later, a gate agent stepped out to inform us that because of a malfunction on the instrument panel of the plane, the flight would not leave until 3:00 a.m.

Dead on my feet, I went across the aisle to another gate that was, along with most of the gates in this giant airport, closed for the night. No flight would be leaving from there for several hours. So I sat down, alone in a sea of empty seats in a quiet area, thinking maybe, just maybe, I might get a few hours of uninterrupted dozing and possibly recover a little from jet lag.

Just as I got somewhat comfortable, a guy walked up. Then he had the audacity to sit down next to me! His shoulder was actually touching my shoulder!

The airport was virtually empty with unoccupied seats everywhere, and he sits down right next to me! I became extremely irritated and a four-letter word entered my mind, and I said it.

"DUDE?"

He responded with an embarrassed smile, and I repeated it again as I pointed to all the empty seats, "DUDE!!!"

"Sir, I'm sorry," he said, "But I saw your desert boots and backpack, and I wondered if you were coming home from this war?"

I could hardly answer for frustration. *His shoulder was touching my shoulder, and he was talking when I wanted to sleep!* Glaring at his shoulder touching mine, hoping he would get the idea that I do not like people touching me, I told him what I do down range in the war zone.

I explained my role as a resiliency coach, working as part of the Comprehensive Soldier Fitness program that is required for the warriors. I told him that my mission was to try to stop some of the suicides, divorces, and the plethora of other tragic consequences in which soldiers find themselves after returning from a devastating war.

When I finished explaining this, out of courtesy I asked, "And where are you coming from?"

He told me he had been to South Texas for the funeral of his very best friend.

I felt my hairpiece stand on end. I could almost feel the rush of blood through my ears, and one of them is plastic. My heart did not know whether to skip a beat or speed up. I felt a shudder go through my body and goose bumps popped up on my arms.

"Your very best friend?" I asked.
"Yes, sir. He was killed."
"In Iraq?"
"Yes, sir."
"Thanksgiving morning?"

"Yes, sir."

"Striker Brigade?"

"Y...e...s, Sir," he stuttered.

His shoulder was not touching mine now. He was leaning back, way back, with his body pressed hard against the far side of his chair. Looking me in the eye, he asked, *"Mister, who **are** you?"*

Without hesitation, I answered, "I am the answer to my own prayer."

Back in Iraq, I had asked God to send someone to comfort the fallen young hero's *very best friend.*

God had answered my prayer.

We both wept. He wept because he realized that in the loss of a best friend, he had met someone who could answer questions to which no one would know the answers without having been there.

I wept because I realized that God had sent me to the backside of the earth to be the right man, in the right place, at the right time to show a *very best friend* that Jesus loves him personally.

This young man was not lost in the events swirling in a world of war, separated by thousands of miles. Through time and space, God found him in an airport.

As we sat together, I was extremely happy that my much-needed rest had been interrupted in order to introduce the best friend of a fallen warrior to a brand-new, *very best Friend* named Jesus.

That is how much Jesus loves each of us. Is one more important than the other ninety-nine? Absolutely not! Everyone is important. There will always be the ninety-nine, and there will always be the one with whom we can share the love of Jesus Christ.

Yeah, God. You can disrupt my down time, any time.

[1] Luke 15:3-5

★   ★   ★

Chapter Ten

You Give Me *Chop-Chop*

"HEY, GI, YOU NUMBER ONE! You give me *chop-chop*?" A smile covered his entire face, as his head appeared for a moment then disappeared behind our boat gunwale only to bob up again as each wave lifted his tiny *sampan*. As quickly as he popped up, he dropped out of sight, like a puppet playing hide-n-seek. I laughed out loud.

So seldom could I laugh about anything those days. War takes a huge toll on the emotions, oftentimes, much more so than on the body. My smile had disappeared with the ravages of war, but this little guy's smile was still there despite the fact that the war was in his backyard, his front yard and living room—if one can call it that.

There were four of us guys, each with personal weapons, plus three giant .50 caliber machine guns (two up front and one aft) and two M60s mid-ship onboard our boat. A Mark18 grenade launcher was mounted with the rear .50 caliber machine gun, and we had enough ammo to start our own war. None of these things, however, bothered the little guy appearing and disappearing with the wash of the water on the starboard side of our floating death machine.

The whole crew saw him at the same time, and it struck us all in the same way. Riotous laughter broke out—a telltale sign of our exhaustion and boredom, a lethal combination when in enemy territory.

The cardinal rule for our defense was to never, *ever,* allow *anyone at anytime* to approach our boat uninvited. Suddenly, the realization that this innocent-looking child could pull the pin on a grenade, readying it to drop into our boat, sent us scrambling to quickly shove him and his canoe-like craft away from us.

My leg was over the edge of the boat, kicking at his sampan, trying to get protective distance between us. A few seconds later, my foot connected with the tiny boat, and I gave it a mighty shove, pitching the smiling boy forward as his craft went into a spinning reverse.

His smile gave way to a look of panic, indicating that if he flipped overboard, he was doomed. I saw the terror in his eyes as he glanced down at the water, but I could not understand the fear. Every child on those rivers in Vietnam could swim like fish. I knew that. Why his panic?

Had he dropped a live grenade into his own boat? Questions were passing through my mind, rapid fire.

Something was very wrong, and my training demanded that I expect the worst. I caught every movement around me. Like a cat, my senses and reflexes were razor-sharp as I lunged for my twin-mounted, mid-ship M60s.

In a flash, I had both guns loaded and trained on the tiny target now drifting slowly backward, watching for the slightest threatening movement. The child did not move at all, much less threateningly. I leaned into my guns, trying to see between the barrels and understand why he remained on the bottom of his sampan. The sickening truth was about to unfold in front of us.

He had tumbled forward neither to retrieve a dropped grenade nor to duck the bullets I thought he was expecting me to spray at him and his boat.

With painfully evident struggle, the little boy was trying to right himself with just his thin arms. He had no legs. The panic was now understandable. At the risk of his life, he wrestled about in the tiny boat trying not to fall overboard. He had tumbled forward because he had no legs to balance himself.

The little guy worked till he pulled himself up onto the board that served as his seat. He dragged dirty rags back over the stumps that extended just a few inches from his hips.

His sampan had ceased its reverse direction and had slowly turned, allowing a long, uninterrupted gaze from his dark eyes into mine—eyes that questioned why I had shoved him away. Eyes that penetrated into my very soul, probing my own fears that I knew were greater than his. Eyes wondering if the index fingers I had on the triggers would show white at the knuckles, pressure determining his fate.

Our eyes locked until the turning boat would no longer allow his gaze to remain. He waited, unmoving, with his little back to me, almost defying me to shoot. My hands relaxed their grip on my weapons, and my legs lowered me to a sitting position on the engine covers where I had stood to shoot. My eyes never left the boy. He waited till the drifting boat turned enough to look back at me again.

The standoff was over when he saw me sitting. His eyes again started their investigation of the situation at hand. Slowly and unthreateningly he lowered his hand to a paddle and began a slow, cautious approach to our boat. The waves still bobbed him up-and-down, in-and-out of sight, each reappearance showing a slightly brighter face until his smile returned full force. His voice repeated the phrase, "Hey, GI, you number one. You give me *chop-chop*?"

I could not remember a time in my life when the simple request for something to eat had caused so much commotion! My heart was still pounding to think that someone had accessed our boat, unsuspected and without fear.

Then I remembered. *He has no legs!*

This war had completely desensitized me to the suffering of others.

Dear God, have I come so far that I have to remind myself of his need?

It was awkward trying to find the proper response. He was hungry. But he had no legs! A little *chop-chop* was not even a band-aid for this child's plight. He needed an orthopedic surgeon, prosthetics, counseling for disabilities, a wheelchair, for heaven's sake!

No. I was wrong.

He needed *chop-chop*, and I did not have any onboard. He needed food for his empty tummy that gnawed at his bones for sustenance. All the legs in the world could not meet his most urgent need. He was hungry, so he did not give his lack of legs a second thought.

Few things in life are more painful to see than the hungry, distended figures of starving people who would trade a handful of hundred dollar bills for a fistful of rice.

I did not know what to do for him. I searched everywhere I

knew to look for something to give to him to eat, but our mission that day was not an overnight patrol requiring a supply of food. Out of the corner of my eye, I happened to catch a reflection of light off the wrapper of a candy bar that had fallen into the engine compartment where we heated food on occasion.

I grabbed the candy bar, wiped the grease from the wrapper, and handed it to the boy. His joy was beyond description. He honestly danced with no legs! He yelped with pleasure and showed off his prize to the other kids who were now making their way toward our boat.

We were about to be surrounded by children with the same appeal. "Hey, GI, you number one. You give me *chop-chop*?"

A brilliant idea passed through my war-weary mind, and it could not have come from any other source except God Himself.

I needed to disperse the crowd, and I did not know of a better way to do that than to jump up yelling, grabbing my big guns, and spinning them around and around. The kids took off in a mad dash for the riverbanks. The sailors on my boat thought I had finally tripped out of my mind.

I knew that the need for food reached beyond the little boy with no legs. The entire village was starving. With the crowd away at a safe distance, I picked up a satchel charge filled with sticks of highly explosive C4. Shaped like a bar of soap, but about a foot long, each was probably equal to a stick of dynamite. I removed the firing mechanism from a grenade and pressed it into the satchel charge, pulled the pin and threw it overboard.

I was never so shocked in all my life as I was when I saw that the charge did not want to sink. It floated for a couple of seconds then sank only enough for its blast to be survivable.

It blew, and the blast picked up the rear end of the eight-ton boat we were on and reversed its course! We all hung on for dear life.

Thankfully, no one was hurt, but wow, what a trip! We were yelling and laughing, but I was waiting for something more important to happen.

I waited. I watched. I hoped.

The river water roiled, and the boat rocked while the guys onboard celebrated our survival.

Then it happened. The blast was right on target, a target I could not see when I tossed the charge.

It was just an idea and a prayer, but it worked. Hundreds of fish started rising to the surface! The river glistened with shinny, silvery fish—stunned and floating belly up.

Every child on the river loaded his boat to the point of sinking. Parents pushed their boats out into the river, joining the children in the largest fish catch in their history. There would be no hunger in the village that night.

A miracle had just happened. A huge school of fish had passed under the boat at the exact time a satchel charge blew. A satchel charge thrown because of an internal nudge, a nudge that had to have been from the Lord, so an entire village could eat.

I could never have known that a school of fish was there, but God knew. My hope was to get a few fish, which was a near certainty. But an entire school of fish? Never! God knew, and because I listened to that internal nudge from Him, a village went to bed with full bellies that night and for several nights thereafter.

The prayer of my heart is that I will always be that sensitive to His nudging.

"…I was hungry and you gave Me something to eat, I was thirsty and you gave Me something to drink, I was a stranger and you invited Me in, I needed clothes and you clothed Me, I was sick and you looked after Me, I was in prison and you came to visit Me.'

"…'Lord, when did we see You hungry and feed You, or thirsty and give You something to drink? When did we see You a stranger and invite You in, or needing clothes and clothe You? When did we see You sick or in prison and go to visit You?'

"The King will reply, 'Truly I tell you, whatever you did for one of the least of these brothers and sisters of mine, you did for Me.'[1]

God sees everything in a big picture that we cannot hope to see. The key is our being sensitive to the Lord in every situation and at all times. It is then that we get to be a part of the unexpected and see things happen that only God can do. There is not a better way to live!

[1] Matthew 25:34-40 *Today's New International Version*

★   ★   ★

Chapter Eleven

Are You Special?

EVER WONDER IF YOU ARE REALLY SPECIAL? Sometimes on television, they show footage of teeming throngs of people on the sidewalks of New York City to give the impression of commonality for all humanity. The implication is that each person is just a nonentity in a mass of nonentities.

For whatever reason, every time I see those pictures, I wonder if I could find myself in that crowd. I may not be able to find me, but I do know this: God can find me. It is impossible to get lost from Him or even to go unnoticed by Him. I take great comfort in the fact that "if I climb to the sky, God is there. If I go underground, God is there! …God would find me in a minute— He's already there, waiting!"[1]

Regardless of how the media may try to lump us together in a sea of humanity, each of us is innately unique.

So, what makes a person special? Is it something he does or does not do? Is it because of someone he knows? Do we assess our "specialness" based on someone else's opinion of us?

Since 9/11/2001, by invitation of the Department of Defense (DOD), I have traveled throughout the world, from our stateside U.S. bases and military installations, to those in many foreign countries. Some of the most life-changing trips for me have been those that have taken me into countries where we are involved in the war on terror.

On a recent trip into Iraq, where the DOD sent me as a resiliency coach, I was fulfilling a request to address the troops as a part of a suicide-prevention tour. Now why would they ask me to do that? Is it because I'm special?

Maybe I am special because I am covered with scars caused by a hand grenade exploding only inches from my face in Vietnam. Sometimes, events outside of our control leave scars on our lives, and sometimes, something very special may come because of them.

Of one thing I am quite certain: I have not been invited by the military to be a resiliency coach for our troops because of my academic achievements. I usually tell people that my special academic achievements can be found in the fact that I was in the top ten percent of the lower one third of my class.

What has contributed to my being special, and to this day makes me special, is that my scarred body is my passport, my visa into places I would never have been invited otherwise. It allows me the privilege of entering the hurting world of those who have been left "special" by the things they have endured.

Many times, we are singled out from the rest of the seemingly normal masses surging down the world's sidewalks by terrible events that mark us for life. Sometimes, being special is not so special after all. I do not like my scars. Most of the time I feel ugly, and if I could erase all these scars, I would do so in a New York minute.

Just one time, I would like to sit in a restaurant and not have someone staring at me, trying to figure out what made me special.

I do not want to be special. I would rather be normal.

Then along comes a moment in my life when my specialness puts me into a situation where, because I am special, everything changes, and I can genuinely give thanks always for all things,[2] including my specialness.

One of those moments happened while on the suicide-prevention tour in Iraq.

I was visiting a hospital on a military base and was sharing my message of resiliency and hope with young warriors who had been wounded in the war. I was able to spend time with them before they were shipped home—before their spouses, friends and family would see them. I wanted to spark resiliency in them before they faced the pressure of new definitions of who they are, the definitions that make them special, whether they want to be special or not.

While there in the hospital, something happened. No expectation or preparation, it just happened.

"Over here, Mr. Roever," the doctor said. "I have someone special I want you to meet."

Of course, I assumed it would be one of our heroes, one of those special guys who had paid the price with loss of limb or traumatic brain injury. ...There are so many things you can lose in a war... things you can never find again...

To my astonishment, it was not one of our soldiers.

He was about 10 years old. You read it correctly. Ten years old.

He had not been injured by an IED (Improvised Explosive Device). No hand grenade had blown up in his face, but you would not know it by looking at him.

He was scarred from head to toe, the little Iraqi boy sitting there in his wheelchair. The terrible scars on his chest had pulled his chin down exactly the way mine had been pulled down from the burns I experienced in Vietnam. To look at me, he had to stand up, which required great exertion, lean far back, which pulled his mouth open, and in that contorted state, he could finally look up far enough to see my face.

Not wanting to cause such extreme discomfort for the little guy, I knelt down in front of him so he could sit down, and we could see eye-to-eye.

In the room with us were several doctors and nurses, as well as my personal security, the General with whom I was traveling, and the little boy's father. An American translator stood close by.

The child stared intently into my eyes. Then I watched as his eyes carefully traced each scar on my face, my neck, my arms, and my hands.

To relieve some of the awkwardness of the moment, I lifted my left hand, which has a stub of a thumb, folded my right index finger over what is left of my right thumb, placed my hands together, and in the old magic trick, I made it look as though I had separated my thumb from my left hand. He thought that was funny, and I got my first smile.

I took off my artificial ear, placed it in the palm of my left hand, raised it up in front of the little boy's face, and said through the translator, "Speak to the hand."

The kid roared in laughter. His little eyes danced in his

scarred face, then his mouth settled into a smile that almost put a halo over his head.

He was so beautiful. I no longer saw his scars. His father stood in awe as he watched his child laugh for the first time since his injury.

Suddenly, the boy began a rapid-fire, animated discourse, his Arabic tongue rattling so quickly it was all that the translator could do to keep up. "My uncle was driving, and we had a terrible crash. He was bleeding, and I could smell gasoline. Suddenly we all burst into flames. I crawled out through the window and escaped the car. I watched my own skin burn and fall off!"

As a resiliency coach, I was in awe of this child. I work extremely hard to get our wounded heroes to talk about their experiences because to do so is the beginning point of healing. When I cannot get a warrior to speak of his experience, he is ultimately sucked into a black hole of despair. Those who do not talk about what happened to them are, almost without exception, the most at risk for suicide.

I realized this little boy was going to make it. He was going to be just fine. The entire medical facility there in Iraq, operated by the U.S. Air Force, was at his beck and call. But the beginning of his success in triumphing in the thing that made him special would be that he could talk about it. No one had warped his thinking by telling him that big boys do not talk about difficult issues.

Then something happened that caught me totally off guard.

At the end of his incredible story, he paused and looked at me, face-to-face, then a cloud came over him. His eyes pooled with tears, and like water over a dam, they poured down his scarred face as he began to weep. He covered his face in shame, his little shoulders heaving.

I did not know what to say. I stood appalled. *Dear God in Heaven, what have I done to break this little boy's heart?*

I begged forgiveness from the child and then from his father.

I said to the staff, "Get me out of here quickly. I don't know what I've done to offend this precious child, but I am so very sorry."

I bowed and apologized again to the father and had turned to walk away when his father grabbed my arm.

"Please don't leave! You have not offended my child. He is not crying in offense; he is weeping for you. He is crying because he realizes that all the pain he has known, you have known. Mr. Roever, he is crying for you!"

Have you ever had a ten-year-old Iraqi boy cry for you? Have you? I think not. I had a ten-year-old Iraqi boy cry for me. I am special. I am very special.

You may not suffer physical scars, but you are special, nonetheless. You are *not* a nonentity in a mass of nonentities—you are special because God created you, a unique, special human being. God says that He knit you together (made you special) in your mother's womb and that you are wonderfully made.[3]

I challenge you to celebrate your specialness as I celebrate mine. Yes, I can honestly, genuinely give thanks always for all things, including my specialness.

[1] Psalm 139:8-10 *The Message* (paraphrased)
[2] Ephesians 5:20
[3] Psalm 139:13-14

★   ★   ★

Chapter Twelve

Tears In The Desert

THE SMALL SPECK ON THE HORIZON GREW LARGER as we approached the border of Syria. As the helicopter began a slow descent, the image below developed into a square shape that finally defined itself clearly. Several hundred men stood in formation at parade rest. They were motionless and focused, despite the ferocious flapping of the American flag and the blowing sand. Angered by the helicopter's giant blades, the swirling sand imitated a tornado in the Iraqi desert.

Following the lead Black Hawk in which the Commanding General and I were riding was an armada of helicopters. As the Black Hawk settled to the ground, it seemed to suggest a respectful approach to the convocation unfolding before us. The vicious shaking, typical of a helicopter landing, and the smell of Jet-A fuel only enhanced the drama in the desert that was about to change my life forever.

I was not yet out of the chopper when I sensed the aura of sadness mixed with honor that lay like a cloud over the troops who, to a man, had not moved a muscle but continued their absolute and stoic silence.

"ATTEN-HUT!"

The order shattered the silence wedged between the landing helicopters. The sudden rattle of hundreds of rifles, jerking from parade rest to a shoulder-high salute, acknowledged the presence of the highest-ranking officer over all of Iraq north of Baghdad.

I took my appointed position, a step behind the General, and watched as other officiating officers took positions with respect to the order of events.

Again, silence fell hard on the desert floor, awaiting the next step in this unfolding scenario. As though an unseen guest had arrived and taken his position front and center, I watched little dust devils dance around my boots, as a gust of wind whipped through the formation.

Now, it seemed, all officiating parties were assembled for the memorial service for Command Sergeant Major Donald Watson. Only two days earlier, the valiant warrior had been killed by an IED (Improvised Explosive Device—in this case, a roadside bomb).

A mindless simpleton, whose wanton waste for a useless cause, pushed the detonator, murdering a courageous man—a recipient of medals for valor and honor. A dad. A mentor.

Words of admiration and recollection spoken by his peers fell on tender ears as this beloved soldier was memorialized. Watching the faces of the soldiers nearest to me, I saw no small shortage of tears as the loss settled into the deepest recesses of their beings. No amount of tears in the desert could roll back the clock. What was done, was done. All that remained were heartache and emptiness.

The defining moment for me came with the initiation of the *Final Roll Call* by the Sergeant Major. The first name called was that of the commanding officer of Northern Iraq. His response was loud and clear. Then followed the name of the second-in-command, then that of the installation commander. In turn, each answered loudly and clearly.

Next came the call, "Command Sergeant Major Donald Watson!"

Silence.

"Command Sergeant Major Donald Watson!"

Silence.

More unnerving still was the third call, "Command Sergeant Major Donald Watson!"

Silence.

Deafening silence.

I could not stop my tears as the unanswered call raced across the desert floor, seeking a backstop to echo a return.

Nothing.

No return.

I waited with baited breath and was lost for a moment in some corridor between now and forever only to be yanked back to reality with the sudden urge to dive for cover.

Incoming fire! I thought.

The twenty-one-gun salute shattered the silence, chasing the Final Roll Call across the desert. Again, the only return was deafening silence.

A third runner chased the salute of the guns. *Taps* began its haunting search for refuge. Musical notes reverberated like the soul seeking a place of rest.

This, surely, will end the memorial service for a fallen hero, I thought, but I was yet to see the conclusion.

Suddenly, out of nowhere, a slap of air attacked my pant leg.

A strong wind swirled about my feet, and what we in Texas call a *dust devil* shot out past me, throwing sand high into the air. It headed straight for the boots, rifle, and helmet of CSM Donald Watson, flinging his dog tags in circles. Then it turned from his memorial and raced across the empty desert space to destinations unknown. I swallowed a chuckle as the thought skimmed through my head, *Yep, a good Command Sergeant Major never misses a roll call!*

As the service came to an end, of one thing I was certain, Command Sergeant Major Donald Watson had already found that place where God-fearing men of honor who have laid down their lives for a brother [1] rest.

No more sacrificing in a lifetime dedicated to the protection of freedom for others.

His reward for honor will not be in medals that tarnish with time. No, his reward for honor will be honor. Our God will give the ultimate honor to whom honor is due. "…Be faithful, even to the point of death, and **I will give you life as your victor's crown**." [2]

[1] John 15:13
[2] Revelation 2:10 *Today's New International Version*

★   ★   ★

Chapter Thirteen

Blood Spilled

MOST PEOPLE WHO HEAR THE NOISE assume that the loud popping from the rotor blades of a helicopter is the result of the incredibly high speed with which the blades travel. In a sense, that is true, but the cause of the unique sound is even more fascinating. The tip of the blade of a helicopter rotor travels faster than the speed of sound, and the rhythmic, loud popping is the result of its repeatedly breaking the sound barrier.

To Vietnam veterans, no helicopter ever built has a more distinct or nostalgic sound than that of the Huey. As for this Vietnam veteran, I do not need the sound of a helicopter blade to send me on a nostalgic trip back to Vietnam.

For me, a barrier of sorts is still being broken. It may not be the sound barrier, but it is a barrier of suppressed recall—memories that are sometimes hard to deal with. Some may call them flashbacks, but in my case, they are just difficult memories.

I know I am not in Vietnam. I know I am not in a firefight. I know I am not floating down the rivers of the dark jungles of Southeast Asia. I am writing this fully aware of who I am, what I have done, from where I have come, and most importantly, where I am going.

Where I am going is called *destination*. How I go about getting there is called destiny. My destination is my choice. Forces and powers over which I have no control often shape my destiny. Inevitable events, be they natural, political, spiritual, physical, or financial, affect my journey.

So what am I trying to say? Along the way in my life, my destiny has been shaped and forged by the flames of sacrifice. Nothing moves me more than those things that have cost life and limb. If you believe in something enough, you will sacrifice whatever is necessary to make it to your destination at the appointed time.

What have been the greatest forces of influence in my life?

Undoubtedly, my service to my country and the sacrifice I made in Vietnam (regardless of whether or not it was ever appreciated by a cruel generation fueled by the media) ranks high on the list.

Far greater, though, than anything that has happened *to* me, is the choice that I made to have a personal relationship with Jesus Christ. His was the ultimate sacrifice: "God rescued us from dead-end alleys and dark dungeons. He's set us up in the kingdom of the Son He loves so much, the Son who got us out of the pit we were in, got rid of the sins we were doomed to keep repeating."[1]

Without Jesus' sacrificing His blood, none of us would have the opportunity to live eternally with Him. I am so grateful to Him and daily thank Him for His sacrifice.

As I have walked among the wounded warriors lying in their hospital beds, I have seen the scars and pain of their sacrifices. One wounded warrior said, "You are the first person ever to say thank you to me." I fought back tears as my imagination and memory filled the gaps for these terribly scarred men.

My thoughts raced back to a time in Iraq where on an LZ (landing zone), I saw a number of medical evacuation helicopters whose rotor blades had gone silent. Each was disgorging blood onto the ground. With water hoses, the ground crew washed wounded soldiers' blood, *life's most precious liquid*, into the Iraqi dirt. Sprays of water and decontaminates washed more blood from gurneys into the desert sands of a country, which we can only hope and pray to God, will someday appreciate the freedom that our warriors' precious blood has bought for them.

From the World Wars, through the Korean and Vietnam wars, to the horrible memories of Somalia, where a wasted sacrifice is hauntingly recalled in the book, *Black Hawk Down*, while blood is still being spilled, sacrifice is forging new destinies. It is sacrifice that has given America a sense of worth.

I travel worldwide, and I have never found a country with a patriotic fervor comparable to that of America. Born out of sacrifice, she is now borne on wings of eagles.

As I walked down the path that day in Iraq, the voices of fallen heroes whose blood soaked the soil seemed to cry out, *Remember me!*

I did.

And I do.

I shall continue to remember the cost of freedom. I remember that on the black, highly polished granite *Wall* in Washington, D.C., nearly sixty thousand names reflect the sacrifice that has forged destinies. Some day in the future, probably long after I am gone, someone will erect a memorial to those who have given their lives in the war on terror.

Why is it so important to remember? Why is it important to show gratitude to those who pay the price for our freedom? The answer is simple.

If we are not thankful, if we do not remember, we will let slip through our fingers what we can never grasp again. Those who will be called upon in the future, the children of today who will fight the wars of tomorrow, will never pay the price for freedom if our nation is not grateful for the liberty we now possess!

God knows I hate war. The only thing I can imagine worse than war is to spinelessly roll over and submit to some ten-horned dictator who would take my freedom away from me and tell me what I can and cannot believe, what I can and cannot say, where I can or cannot go, or what I can or cannot be.

Taking my boots off that day in Iraq and carefully skirting the bloodstained soil, I said to the doctors and their staff who had escorted me to this LZ, "We need to put a fence around this place. We need to build a memorial.

"We need to announce to all who pass this hallowed ground that this is a holy place where sacrificial blood has been spilled. Then perhaps someday, Iraqi children will remember that someone loved them enough to die for them."

I remember another place that still brings tears to my eyes— a place of reverence—a place where blood was shed and a monument was raised. It was a place where a Man paid the ultimate sacrifice to buy my freedom.

"When you were stuck in your old sin-dead life, you were incapable of responding to God. God brought you alive—right along with Christ! Think of it! All sins forgiven, the slate wiped clean, that old arrest warrant canceled and nailed to Christ's cross. He stripped all the spiritual tyrants in the universe of their sham authority at the Cross and marched them naked through the streets." [2]

Ah, what sweet victory we have in Jesus! Because His blood was spilled, we can choose to live in freedom.

[1] Colossians 1:13-14 The Message
[2] Colossians 2:13-15 The Message

★   ★   ★

Chapter Fourteen

Chieu Hoi

IN JUNE OF 1971, THE MUSIC SEEMED DISTANT, almost hollow, as if I were in a long tunnel, spiraling back in time, spanning the last few years with an uncanny recall of the events so vivid in my memory. The odors were real, as if emitted in the very room where I knelt. A massive hand pressed down upon my scabbed head, which was devoid of large patches of hair that would never grow back.

Kneeling there, my mind replayed the memories. The smell of

decomposing bodies and the acrid odor of gunpowder dueled within my head for control of my presence of mind. My mind, which was coursing back to the rivers of Vietnam...

Idling engines gurgled softly in the water as we bobbed up-and-down in the wash of our own wake. Our senses on high alert, white knuckles gripped the gun mounts fore and aft on our gunboat.

We waited.

Not daring to look away, my eyes scoured the riverbank for the first signs of movement of the enemy.

A staggering silhouette with hands clasped together behind his head struggled out of the dense foliage that grew along the bank of the river. His black pajamas glistened with dark red patches, which were spreading like an oil slick on water. He muttered something then fell to one knee, still keeping his hands high.

"Chieu Hoi! Chieu Hoi," he kept saying.

I knew what the words meant. They were words of surrender. Words of a dying man caught in deadly crossfire. Words uttered in pain of soul as well as body.

The world had closed in on him, leaving him exhausted from sleepless nights and a poor diet. Now bleeding and trembling in pain, he knelt—totally at the mercy of his captors, men from a foreign place with a foreign speech, men as confused as he was, wondering why the death, why the pain, why the war?

Almost inaudible, the words, *"Chieu Hoi, Chieu Hoi,"* continued to slip from his trembling lips.

Tears ran down his face from the unrelenting pain that pressed him to the earth, like the heavy hand I now felt on my own head. The weight of the hand pressed so hard on me, I felt as though my back would break under the weight of it.

Tears and more tears flowed, followed by strains of music fading in and out, as my mind washed between past and present. Words sung softly by the robed choir cradled the prayer so urgently being prayed over me by the man whose hand crowned my head. All this emotion... The memories bled through the cracks of dried scar tissue in my mind. Is this the past or present? Is it 1969 or 1971?

"Chieu Hoi, Chieu Hoi!"

These words of surrender spasmodically interrupted the music and prayers. The visage of a broken man of war, bleeding and wounded, knowing that the last battle of his life had been fought, and surrender was the better part of valor, slumped over and breathed his last.

"Chieu Hoi, Chieu Hoi," now formed on my own trembling lips as tears soaked my face, leaving the taste of salt in my mouth. The words of surrender were now being uttered on this, the night of my ordination into ministry. I was on my knees in surrender to the Highest Power—God Himself—

willingly, gladly saying to Him, "Whatever You want me to do, wherever You want me to go, whatever You want me to say, I am willing, Lord."

Many years have passed since my dad placed his hands on my head, and, in the presence of a thousand witnesses, prayed the Ordination Prayer of Ministry that has followed me all my life. ...More than forty years since my lips uttered those words of unconditional surrender to the will of God for my life. ...more than forty years of full-time, uninterrupted ministry that confirm two important facts: 1) Dad's prayer was answered; 2) my Lord and Master, Christ Jesus, accepted the terms of my unconditional, *Chieu Hoi,* surrender.

Some of you are scratching your heads and wondering what surrender to God really means.

I like the way the Apostle Paul explained it to the people in Rome. "So here's what I want you to do, God helping you: Take your everyday, ordinary life—your sleeping, eating, going-to-work, and walking-around life—and place it before God as an offering. Embracing what God does for you is the best thing you can do for Him. Don't become so well adjusted to your culture that you fit into it without even thinking. Instead, fix your attention on God. You'll be changed from the inside out. Readily recognize what He wants from you, and quickly respond to it. Unlike the culture around you, always dragging you down to its level of immaturity, God brings the best out of you, develops well-formed maturity in you."[1]

The years since I said *Chieu Hoi* to God have been the most exciting years that any man could possibly ever want to live. Jesus, Who captured me with His love, has, by that same love, set me free!

When I come to the end of my life, knowing that the last battle has been fought, with my final breath my words will still be *Chieu Hoi*—I surrender.

"The person in right standing (absolute surrender) before God...*really lives.*"[2]

1 Romans 12:1-2 *The Message*
2 Romans 1:17 *The Message*

★   ★   ★

Chapter Fifteen

Eagles Summit Ranch

THE WIND WHISTLED THOUGH MY HELMET as I kicked into a lower gear, the pull of Hardscrabble Pass severe against the motorcycle's transmission. I glanced up at the beautiful cliffs reaching to ten thousand feet. Then looking across the deep canyons, my eyes were drawn to a peak that looks remarkably like an arrowhead. Perhaps the arrow itself was pointing me in the right direction.

"Go west, young man, go west," someone once said. And

west was the way I sensed the arrowhead was directing me. My engine chugged a time or two, so I downshifted again. The sharp hairpin curves pulled me higher and higher. After a long labor by the engine and my shifting gears multiple times, I leveled off onto a high desert plain. There before me, on Colorado's Highway 96, jutting much higher than the plain on which I traveled, were beautiful snow-capped mountains. Mountains, which on just the right day, at just the right time, and with just the right angle of sun through the earth's atmosphere, reflect the most beautiful red-rose color.

I felt the breath sucked from my nostrils. A spirit of joy swept over my soul as I beheld the *Sangre de Cristo Mountains.*

The conquistadors, I am told, passed through here centuries ago, and with just the right elements, the reflection of the sun on the face of the mountains was so red they exclaimed, "Sangre de Cristo!" (Blood of Christ!) Since that time, the mountain range has been known only by that name. The Sangre de Cristo Mountains are some of the most beautiful in all of the Rocky Mountain Range.

As I cruised through the Sangre de Cristo Mountains that day, I think I remember vowing that I would return someday. That I would come back to look for the breath that I had lost, to discover why my heart raced, and to feel the wind in my face again. And I did.

I came back.

I came back to where something so marvelous had happened. Like a drug addict, I sought another high. Some call it a Rocky Mountain high. I call it a glimpse of the Most High. God was speaking to me, and many years later, what He said would be fulfilled.

★   ★   ★

We backed the people mover up to the paved parking area at Eagles Summit Ranch, located high in the Wet Mountains overlooking the Wet Valley. The Ranch stares straight at the Sangre de Cristo Mountain Range with some of its gorgeous peaks soaring over 14,000 feet. Almost every window in the Eagles Summit Lodge has a view of these special "Blood of Christ" Mountains.

I swung the tailgate open and grabbed the bags of a great young warrior, BJ, who lost both his legs in Iraq when a roadside bomb exploded.

"I'll take your bags to the top floor. You ride the elevator," I said.

Striding along on his prosthetic limbs, his instantaneous response was, "No Sir! I don't want to ride in no stinkin' elevator! I'll take the stairs, Mr. Roever."

I fired back just as quickly, "No Sir! You ride this elevator, Mr. BJ. You are my hero. I will take the bags to the top floor."

That was not the end of it.

"No Sir," he said again, "I'll take the stairs. I don't want to ride no elevator."

Thinking perhaps he was balking because he was terrified of the claustrophobia of an elevator, I resisted further debate. I said, "Okay, I'll ride the elevator, 'cause fat boys like elevators anyway."

I got in the elevator, pushed the button, and beat him to the top floor, only to hear a crack, a thud, then bump... bump...bump...bump.

I looked over the banister. BJ did not make it to the top.

Somewhere he had missed a step, and down he went. Both prosthetic legs came off and crashed to the bottom floor, one to the left and one to the right. For a moment my heart stopped. *Is he okay?*

Before I could voice my concern, a sheepish grin eased across BJ's face, and I asked, "Hey, BJ. Can you say *el-e-va-tor*?"

"Yeah, Mr. Roever," he said. "It was my fault. I was running the stairs backwards."

These are the people who come to Eagles Summit Ranch. Young heroes. United States fighting warriors who have laid it all on the line.

Some have lost legs. Some have lost arms. And for some who have survived, their memory has gone away as well. So often they come to Eagles Summit Ranch beat up, torn up, and ripped asunder.

No doubt, the enemy took their legs, severed their arms, and stole their memory, but for some special reason, the enemy just could not strip them of their spirits. There is just something about our fighting warriors. Their bodies may be wounded and their minds tormented, but something inside just will not surrender.

No Sir. No white flags here. When they come to this ranch, they go to sleep tired from a long day of activities and training. At sunrise, they peek out the windows, and reflected in their eyes is the Sangre de Cristo Mountains.

There are so many good places for contemplation at Eagles Summit Ranch. Places to where this old beat-up Vietnam veteran can slip away and sit down, face-to-face, with some of these young, beat-up veterans, and speak heart-to-heart, with pulses racing and tears sometimes washing the windows of their souls.

Whenever the unique instances of the opening of the heart arise, we are there for the warriors. We never know when it will happen, maybe on the peak of a distant mountain or sitting in front of the fireplace in the great room of the lodge. Somewhere, sometime, for whatever reason, they feel comfortable enough to empty their souls and speak of the unspeakable. They reach into painful spots to pick at the scabs and make them bleed.

I think that breeze I speak of so often races through the halls of the lodge. It blows across the plains of their minds, then like smoke, it dissipates, and, along with it, all the attending horrors and the post-traumatic stress that has filled their very beings.

Hope and vision replace despair and despondency. "I can make it," becomes an often-spoken theme.

"If you can make it, Mr. Roever, then so can I."

Eagles Summit Ranch was not built for a vacation hideaway for these warriors. It stands as a shining beacon on a mountain, pointing the way to a better future. The classroom study at the ranch is intense. The warriors learn about themselves and others. They rediscover those incredible assets that made them great warriors and that will now make them more than conquerors.

Eagles Summit Ranch was built out of the tragedy in my own life, and its focus truly became sharp and distinct as I exited a freeway in Fargo, North Dakota, one day. As we came to the end of the off ramp, an old Vietnam veteran held up a sign with scribbled writing, declaring he was stranded in Fargo.

He was not stranded in Fargo; he was stranded in time. He was stranded in self-pity, judged now to be too old, and the time far too late to change and start over. A thought went through my mind. Two simple words, and I saw two simple words in giant bold print.

NEVER AGAIN

Never again will we allow Americans to fall into the septic tank of self-righteousness and permit the decimation of character of our warriors returning home from battle.

Never again will this nation allow our warriors to return to chants of "Baby Killers" from imbeciles wrapped in their arrogance—people who continue to thrive in their money-making endeavors while riding on the backs of those who bought their freedom and allowed them the privilege of living in a free society. Do not talk to me about the value of their freedom of expression.

At Eagles Summit Ranch, we have paid a great price for freedom of expression. Today, returning warriors benefit from the sacrifices of yesterday's heroes, the Vietnam veterans. Because of what they suffered, today's warriors can come home with pride and honor and, most certainly, opportunity. God bless the Vietnam veterans.

God bless the young warriors as they come to Eagles Summit Ranch. They are not grasping for straws, they are reaching for scepters, taking hold of the pride of a nation. With chins high and eyes elevated, they are gazing at the horizon, knowing their best days are yet to come.

On the wings of Eagles Summit Ranch, they learn to fly. "He gives strength to the weary and increases the power of the weak. Even youths grow tired and weary, and young men stumble and fall; but those who hope in the LORD will renew their strength. They will soar on wings like eagles; they will run and not grow weary, they will walk and not be faint."[1]

---

[1] Isaiah 40:29-30 *Today's New International Version*

★　　★　　★

127

Chapter Sixteen

Swapping Faces

"WE NEED TO SWAP FACES," I TOLD THE GUY. We laughed because we knew that no one would know the difference!

It is almost scary to meet someone who looks a lot like yourself. He was even my age...when I was injured. The difference is, when I met him, my injury was over thirty years old. His was only months old.

My injury happened while I was on a small boat in the jungles of Vietnam. His happened while he was on a helicopter over the deserts of Iraq.

I was hit by a hand grenade which blew away most of my face. He was on a Black Hawk helicopter, which was hit by another Black Hawk.

When hand grenades explode inches from your face or helicopters collide in midair, no one is supposed to live. Yet, there we sat, laughing and telling each other our stories.

He served with the U.S. Army's 101st Airborne. I served with the U.S. Navy's Special Warfare Unit, the Brown Water Black Berets. We came from two different worlds. But both of us fought for the same cause—the cause of peace in a terrified world.

I scanned the room. One man in his early twenties sat in a wheelchair with his wife and two small children by his side. An uncertain future had left them with grim faces. The two adorable and perfectly behaved children somehow sensed the reality that challenged the entire family.

Near the back of the room sat a lieutenant colonel. He was missing a leg. Eight other wounded warriors filled the room and waited patiently to hear the words of encouragement that I would share. The 101st Airborne had once again kept their promise by bringing their wounded warriors together for mentoring and ministry. My motto for these young heroes: *You can come without legs. I'll get you back on your feet.*

After the presentation, soldiers lined up to sign up. "Teach me your skills, Mr. Roever. I want to tell the world my story of how Christ delivered me. Can I go to the mentoring center in Colorado with you?"

My eyes blinded by tears, I handed this hero a pen, "Sign here. The future is yours, and I will help you build it."

I watched as bent, broken, and scarred fingers somehow gripped the ballpoint pen and a shaky hand reaches far into tomorrow with each printed letter of his name. We are here, pulling that hand forward from the quagmire of a painful history into a golden future.

For many of us, it still lies fresh on our minds. It is not pleasant to recall when the broken hearts and hands of returning Vietnam veterans reached forward, and no one was there. There was no firm grip to pull those returning warriors from the ruin of hopelessness.

I could not sleep another night, nor would I care to live another day, if I thought for a moment we would repeat history's evil by an unrepentant nation—ingrates actually, who would bring these soldiers home from war the way America brought home the Vietnam vets. Not now! Not again! Not ever!

The message I am constantly driving home to young warriors is, we might be "...hedged in, pressed on every side, troubled and oppressed in every way, but not cramped or crushed; we suffer embarrassments and are perplexed and unable to find a way out, but not driven to despair;...pursued, persecuted and hard driven, but not deserted to stand alone; we are struck down to the ground, **but never struck out and destroyed**;"[1]

Our victory cry? "...Amid all these things we are more than conquerors and **gain a surpassing victory** through Him Who loved us!"[2]

[1] 2 Corinthians 4:8-9 *Amplified Bible*
[2] Romans 8:37 *Amplified Bible*

★　★　★

Chapter Seventeen

Little Lambs

WHEN I WAS FIVE-YEARS-OLD, I accompanied my mother to the home of a parishioner from the church my parents pastored. The lady was ill, and Mom and I had gone to pray for her. When I walked into her house, I saw a picture of Jesus on the wall, and it was unlike any I had ever seen.

In those days, it seemed everybody had a picture of Jesus hanging on a wall in the family home. None of the pictures were exactly the same, so as a child, I was a bit bewildered, wondering what Jesus really looked like.

It was not the picture of Jesus that so took me by surprise that day. It was what Jesus was doing in the picture that I did not understand. Jesus was holding in one of His arms a small lamb whose broken leg had been splinted and wrapped in white gauze. Jesus' other hand and forearm were lying gently on the lamb's back, holding it firmly in place.

Not long ago, a wounded warrior shared with me his heartbreaking, touching story of suffering. His arm is mangled, and the muscle tissue is horribly damaged. In addition to the damage to the muscle tissue, the bones in the arm had been broken, the shoulder dislocated, and some of the bones in his hand are missing. Accompanying these injuries is severe nerve damage with its own assault of problems. I estimate his arm is only ten-percent usable.

Of his own volition, the young man made this statement, "I would have been better off if they had amputated my arm and given me a prosthesis. Missing arms don't hurt."

Out of this unrestrained statement of candid honesty, he arrived at a realization without a conclusion. "It's useless. But for what purpose?"

My mind went back to the picture I had seen as a child of Jesus holding that little lamb with a broken and useless leg.

It was *Jesus* holding the lamb.

134

It was not Dr. Kevorkian, dubbed *Dr. Death* by the media, who probably would have said, "Let's put the animal down. He's going to die anyway. After all, it only has three good legs."

It was not the finest physician in orthopedic care at one of our military hospitals who cradled the lamb in his arms. *It was Jesus!*

Which begs the question, *Why did Jesus wrap and splint the leg when He could have healed it?* After all, Jesus raised the dead; He opened blind eyes. Jesus is the Miracle Man, the Son of God Who can walk on water.

Why did He splint the leg of the little lamb when He could have healed it?

As a five-year-old boy, I looked up at my mother, a woman who had already begun to enter what would be years of horrific suffering that eventually would leave her in a fetal position for a decade before she drew her last breath. A woman who was the best communicator I have ever known, who would be suddenly left speechless by a stroke and never utter another word. This is the woman into whose face I looked and asked, "Mommy, why did Jesus put a splint on the leg when He could have healed it?"

Her insight was profound as she answered my question, "A lamb with a broken leg cannot run away and must be carried in the arms of God."

I spoke from my heart to the young warrior when I told him

that for the rest of his life, his arm would remind him of his dependency on Jesus, just as my scarred face continually reminds me to hide behind the image of Christ.

That wounded warrior's arm will never be used normally again, but the arms of God that cradle him will also sustain and defend him because he can no longer fend for himself.

"Listen to Me, (says the Lord)... I've been carrying you on My back from the day you were born, and I'll keep on carrying you when you're old. I'll be there, bearing you when you're old and gray. I've done it and will keep on doing it, carrying you on My back, saving you."[1]

"...I haven't dropped you. Don't panic. I'm with you. There's no need to fear for I'm your God. I'll give you strength. I'll help you. I'll hold you steady, keep a firm grip on you."[2]

[1] Isaiah 46:3-4 *The Message*
[2] Isaiah 41:9-10 *The Message*

★   ★   ★

Chapter Eighteen

Suffering Heroes

WHAT SCARS DO YOU BEAR FROM YOUR PAST? A past you cannot change, a past the enemy of your soul seems to always want to use to taunt you. Some of you were sexually abused when you were young, and, just as devastating, some of you were ignored by the people you love. Others of you were given all the love necessary to carry you through the difficult years just like I was.

One thing is certain: *everybody suffers.*

Many, if not all, of my heroes have been people who suffered. One such sufferer was my mother, who from the day of my birth, began a physical decline that progressively worsened. At the time of her death, I had never known anyone to suffer as much as she did and yet never complain.

Another hero of mine is General Robinson Risner. For seven-and-a-half years, Gen. Risner was a prisoner-of-war in North Vietnam in a brutally inhumane prison, nicknamed the *Hanoi Hilton* by the American POWs held there. It was in this hellhole that the North Vietnamese tortured captured servicemen, mostly American pilots who had been shot down, with methods indescribably cruel. Among other things, Gen. Risner was beaten, starved, and his arms were tied behind his back, then pressure was applied to the bindings until his chest literally split open. On more than one occasion, he was at the point of death.

Even though incarcerated and under threat of his life, Gen. Risner used a form of Morse code to tap out Bible verses on the concrete walls of his cell. The messages of the love of God and hope in Jesus were transmitted from cell-to-cell by the faint sound of a tap ... tap ... tap, infusing fellow prisoners with the will to survive.

In the courtyard of the Air Force Academy in Colorado Springs, a statue of Gen. Risner stands as a monument to a great hero—a man who suffered!

Then there is my greatest Hero of all... Who, being the Son of

God and having the power to stop what was happening to Himself, did not. He was beaten, tortured, and killed. One may find His statue in a courtyard somewhere, but far more important is that His resurrected image is etched deeply into the fabric of our lives. This Man was scarred for the love of us all, and He was obedient unto death.

What about heroes like you?

"I'm no hero," you say. Yet some of you suffer in ways beyond my understanding. You suffer quietly without complaining.

My list of heroes includes single parents, mothers and fathers who, though stretched almost to the breaking point, still find time to nurture their children and teach them about God. My list includes divorcees who, having endured the unspeakable pain of a broken heart and a shattered relationship, have not blamed nor hated God.

Then there are those who have suffered physical wounds. In themselves, some wounds are not serious enough to cause death. However, if they are left unattended with no cleansing, no stitches, no healing salve, the hemorrhaging and infection can cause what the wound itself did not do, inevitable death.

The same is true for wounded hearts and souls. Some people live with "wounds and welts and open sores, not cleansed or bandaged or soothed with oil."[1] Left to fester, wounds of the heart will kill.

The first step in healing for a wounded soul is to choose to forgive. Forgiving is not based on feeling; it is a choice. We choose to forgive because we do not want to be bound to and controlled any longer by whomever or whatever has hurt us.

When you heal, the scar that follows will be a flashing neon sign, telling the world, "Hey, look, I got hurt, but I got well. I survived my wound. And here's my scar to prove it."

The whole world gets hurt, but only the ones who are healed, only the man with the scar, the woman with the scar, the teenager with the scar can say, "I know how you feel. Let me help you get through this."

Jesus does that with us. "He comes alongside us when we go through hard times, and before you know it, He brings us alongside someone else who is going through hard times so that we can be there for that person just as God was there for us. We have plenty of hard times that come…but no more so than the good times of His healing comfort—we get a full measure of that, too."[2]

There are two kinds of suffering: suffering for a cause and suffering without a cause. Pain without gain is the ultimate loss.

What about you? Are your scars being wasted? Let me shout it loudly for all to hear: *all human suffering, regardless of its source, can be turned in a positive direction.*

Do not walk away from Christ. Instead, run to Him! Do not blame God when you are hurting; He is the One who can help you. Do not desert your faith; use it to find yourself, and in finding yourself, find complete healing through God for your body and soul. "It's in Christ that we find out who we are and what we are living for. Long before we first heard of Christ and got our hopes up, He had His eye on us, had designs on us for glorious living, part of the overall purpose He is working out in everything and everyone."[3]

In a restaurant one day, some young people were ridiculing my disfigurement, and I became intensely humiliated as they mocked my scars. Suddenly the Spirit of Jesus in me began to speak to my heart.

"You don't like them laughing at you?"

I thought, *No, I don't.*

He said, "It was to set them free. You suffered for them, and the scars they laugh at were for them."

"Yes, Lord."

"You don't like it, do you? It's not fair is it?"

"Lord, it's not fair."

Then He said to me, "Now you know how I feel."

Could I have known what I know through riches? Would fame or power have taught me the lessons I have learned? Could I have understood the heart of Christ through success?

No. Only through these scars, wounds that are healed, have

I come to know, to love, to adore, and to understand Jesus Christ.

Your pain need not be wasted. Let it lead you to an understanding of Christ Jesus Who was wounded for our transgression and bruised for our iniquities.[4]

He knows how we feel. Let Him show you His scars. He stands with palms up. Look at His hands. Look at His feet. See the wound in His side. He suffered all of that so you could be healed.

When you are healed, do not waste your scars. Let your healing be the means of bringing healing to someone else's life. Let your tragedy become a triumph for you. Be a hero as you stand tall in your faith.

Sometimes we feel that God has rejected us and Jesus has thrown us away. When you think that way, just remember that Jesus suffered for us, He was scarred for us, and He WILL NOT discard that for which He has sacrificed his life!

[1] Isaiah 1:6 *Today's New International Version*
[2] 2 Corinthians 1:3-4 *The Message*
[3] Ephesians 1:11-12 *The Message*
[4] Isaiah 53:5 *King James Version*

★　★　★

142

Chapter Nineteen

I Am At Peace

I only regret that I have but one life
to lose for my country. - Nathan Hale

"**M**R. ROEVER, GIVE ME ONE GOOD REASON…uh…just one good reason why I should not pull this trigger."

I had heard that voice on other occasions when he was strung out on prescription meds, generously prescribed by military doctors, to mask his pain. The injuries sustained in his body were nothing compared to the suffering incurred in his soul when he survived the blast that took out his best friend and several other members of his squad. Traumatic physical injury and survivor's guilt weighed heavily upon the psyche of the young soldier on the other end of the telephone line.

In my mind, I could see him gingerly caressing the weapon, knowing full well he was capable of squeezing the trigger. His deliberation was to somehow end the continuing nightmares and onslaughts from hell that had captured his consciousness. He was desperate. He was confused. He was hopeless.

Gently, I said, "Tomorrow... You have tomorrow." I reasoned with him and shared with him the hope that only Christ can bring to a distraught spirit.

Before long, I heard the quiet sobs of a broken heart relinquishing the pain of the past, casting the cares of his life onto the shoulders of the only One who could sustain his burden.

Post Traumatic Stress is normal. It is a natural occurrence in the lives of those who have served in combat situations. It is not atypical, nor is it to be viewed as a weakness; hence, I do not use the "D" word...*Disorder.*

Like a self-fulfilling prophecy, the *D word* insinuates chaos. Make no mistake—there is confusion and mental pain, but I do not believe, nor do I accept for myself or for other warrior friends that *disorder* is an accurate definition of our condition.

Stress…yes. Order gone wild…no.

Recently a bystander overheard me ask the U.S. Surgeon General, "Sir, why do we use the term *disorder* when describing the state-of-mind of our wounded warriors?"

The bystander, a mental-health professional with a major medical insurance agency, piped up before the Surgeon General could answer, "If you don't label it a disorder, insurance will not cover the cost for treatment."

That does not work for me.

That self-fulfilling prophecy only prepares a warrior for failure. I want to be prepared for success by believing that if something is broken, it can be fixed with time, love, purpose, and the power that comes from God. I do not believe it can be fixed with Oxycontin, Percocet, alcohol, or any other substance that could possibly make matters worse by spiraling in a whole new set of problems.

Let me take you back in my own life—way back to January of 1969 in Vietnam. It was hot in January. It was hot all the time, but the climate of my soul was about to soar to the pinnacle of my spiritual thermometer.

First, let us go back even further, all the way back to the innocence of my childhood and youth—as unblemished as a virgin.

When my peers would offer a cigarette, I would just say, "No."

145

When they asked why not, I easily answered, "I don't know how to smoke."

I never saw a cigarette between the fingers of my father's hands, nor in the lips of my mother. Smoking was never introduced to me as a habit, much less a lifestyle. Oh sure, I saw people smoking in public, but I never saw it in the privacy of our home. And my father's wisdom on the perils of smoking, which was scoffed at by many of that day, has come full circle.

Going to movies was taboo with my family. As a child, I never saw a horror movie. Even innocent black and white television shows were not permitted in our home. My forward-thinking parents feared where the media would lead this country, so I never focused on the bigger-than-life heroes that Hollywood created.

The same was true for alcohol, drugs, and sex outside of a marriage relationship. People called our family prudes because we were not hip with television. We were not hip with the movies. We were just plain "uncool."

So how could a young man, as innocent as I was, enter into the Naval Special Warfare Division, and possibly hope to survive in the wild and wicked days of the 1960's where sex, drugs, and alcohol abuse were rampant? In the *Golden Triangle* of Southeast Asia, especially in Vietnam, sex, drugs, and alcohol were as commonly discussed as M16s, Claymore mines, and B-40 rockets.

146

Was it even remotely possible for an innocent young man to be exposed to such and survive?

Yes.

It was, and I did. My anchor was rooted in concrete moral standards, ethical righteousness, and unflawed character. All were set firmly on the foundation of God and family.

It is important to realize that the defense of the defenseless, the help of the helpless, and the giving of hope to the hopeless are the most "Jesus things" a man will ever do. *To lay down one's life for a friend*[1], Jesus declared, is the highest form of love. If a policeman (or a soldier) has the power to intervene in a volatile situation, and an innocent is killed, does the policeman assume the guilt of killing that innocent person?

When the Bible says, "You shall not kill," it speaks of murder; otherwise, taking the life of an ant, a flea, a bird, or the slaying of an animal for food would not be permitted. Murder is wrong.

Putting one's life on the line to stop terrorists from terrorizing and murdering, even when it means taking the life of the terrorist, is an honorable thing. I can honestly say I am thankful that I had the honor to serve my country and defend innocent people who would most certainly have been slaughtered at the hands of the enemy.

My cut-short tour of duty in Vietnam began in January of 1969. The worst-of-times in war for me came when we had to do body counts after horrendous firefights and exchanges of hostilities with the Viet Cong. One specific tally, my first, that plagues me to this day happened in an area we called *Devil's Hole*. The sight remains as vivid for me now as it was then.

I remember how the flesh of my index finger turned white from pressing against the curved lever of the trigger. Surely, the oily indentions and crevices of my fingerprint were engraved into the metal. Before the initial squeeze of the trigger, I was convinced that I would throw down my gun and run at the sound of the first round of fire from the enemy. Just the opposite happened. I used the weapon and fought for my life. I fought for the lives of my comrades-in-arms. I fought for my nation and its democratic way of life. And I fought for the Republic of South Vietnam in hopes of preserving freedom for their people.

I have not the slightest regret for my actions. The memories of the short time I spent in the Mekong Delta are still deeply engrained in the backlogs of my mind. War and remembrance are not strange bedfellows.

Every man must deal in his own way with his own conscience about the eternal question of a truly *just* or *unjust* war. While the Gulf War under George H.W. Bush was unanimously heralded a justified war, the Vietnam War under Lyndon Johnson was discredited. People rioting in the streets during the Vietnam era were replaced by yellow ribbons and homecoming parades for those who served in the Middle East.

How does an "unjustified" war go full bore and a Vietnam veteran say that he has no regrets?

There is a simple answer for such a complex question: I am at peace with myself. It is *my* conscience and *my* perceptions. It is not yours. It is not a fellow warrior's. It is not politics. My justification lies at ease within the confines of my heart.

Vietnam veterans were called baby killers, but I never killed a child. We were called warmongers, but I have always hated war. I still despise war. It rapes. It plunders. It dismembers. Every scar on my body is verification of that. But I love freedom! My love of freedom is barely more measurable than my hatred of war, just enough never to want a war, but sufficient enough to fight for the ideals of one nation, under God, indivisible, with liberty and justice for all.

Was the transition from the innocence of a peace-loving family to the violence and horrors of war easy? Not in the slightest.

After the bodies were counted that day at Devil's Hole, I returned to our forward operation base, which was a floating barge in the middle of a Mekong Delta river. On that barge was our housing, our cocoon from the heat—a clean, air-conditioned space that could not turn down the temperature of my burning heart nor of my charring soul. When I put my face into my pillow, I screamed a phrase that I had heard as a child, as a young Boy Scout, "For God and Country...for God and Country...for God and Country!"

The next time I would scream into a pillow would be at Brooke Army Medical Center in San Antonio, Texas. With almost half my skin blown off my body, my face charred to the skull, no hair, one ear, and one nostril, I buried my face deep in a pillow and screamed.

I do not remember saying "For God and Country" that day. I was in much-too-much pain. It hurt like hell...not in the cursing sense, but in the literal sense. Was this my hell for the fight I had fought? Was this hellish pain coursing through my body in waves, raging from nausea to hallucination, my reward?

The last breath from my lungs exhaled into the pillow, which served as the muffler for my crying soul. Of course, when you run out of breath, you feel like you have run out of time. You feel like you have run out of hope, and there was nothing to relieve the pain. That is called absolute, total despair.

I lifted my head to suck in air.

Wait a minute...why suck in air? Why not go ahead and die?

Do you know that it is impossible for a human being to hold his breath until he dies? It is impossible because every cell in the brain is dictating to every nerve in the body, telling the lungs to inhale, to suck in air because a human body is wired to live, not to die.

Raising my head and gasping for air, my one good eye saw the burned skin from my face attached firmly to the fibers of the pillowcase. Gone with my face was every sliver of hope. If there was a shred of hope, I deemed it gone.

Remembrance can be a friend or an enemy.

My history must not dictate the parameters of my future. Rather, my history has very carefully steered me in the right direction toward the future. Reality is focused and sharpened by pain, relieved by prayer, and secured with hope and the certain knowledge that everything in my life—good, bad or ugly, will turn to the good of my own salvation, and that nothing ever planned against me from the pit of despair or the pit of hell, can overcome the firm foundation on which this innocent life was set.

As I travel the highways of this nation I love, I marvel at the wonders of God's creation. When I enter a mountain range and view stark, barren stones ascending to the heavens, I am in awe. On more than one occasion, I have been amazed to see that out of the smallest of cracks, with not the slightest hope of its ever being tended by a gardener, grows a small cedar with dark green branches bent away from the wind.

How could it possibly survive? The angle of its development has been shaped by the pressures against it, and somehow it stands.

The tree would never have survived in soft soil in a clay pot on a back porch—coddled, watered regularly, shaded from the sun, with nary a wisp of wind to batter it. Oh no, not this cedar. It is firmly intrenched in the rock of its salvation. Its strength lies in the fact that it has been buffeted by adversity.

Yes, I have seen war, and most certainly have known God's guiding hand throughout my life. All the buffeting by adversity that I have experienced has made me a better man. I do not dwell on the days and years of pain, nor do I contemplate on what might have been. My broken places have made me stronger through the tempering of fire.

I have learned to "triumph in my troubles and rejoice in my sufferings, knowing that pressure and affliction and hardship produce patient and unswerving endurance. And endurance develops maturity of character...And character of this sort produces the habit of joyful and confident hope of eternal salvation. *Such hope never disappoints...*"[2]

Because I have learned to triumph through my tragedies, I am now able to guide other wounded warriors, like the young man on the other end of the telephone line, toward hope-filled futures and wholeness after the ravages of war.

I have hope because I know "All things work together and are fitting into a plan for good...for those who love God and are called according to His design and purpose."[3]

I am at peace.

[1] John 15:13 *New King James*
[2] Romans 5:3-5 *Amplified Bible*
[3] Romans 8:28 *Amplified Bible*

★   ★   ★

Chapter 20

Pulling the Pin on Unforgiveness

THROUGH THE YEARS, I have met thousands of Vietnam veterans, and I have lived to see this truth. The Vietnam veterans who still hold bitterness, hatred and unforgiveness toward any entity that they have perceived to be the cause of their suffering and pain (the communists, Lyndon Johnson, Jane Fonda, Agent Orange, etc.) are wrecks. They inevitably exhibit haggard faces and hollow eyes. Often they have serious health complications due to substance abuse. Their downward spiral has put them on paths to spousal abuse and the fostering of dysfunctional families.

For them, the unforgiveness has been so internalized that the enemy in Vietnam, now decades later, has finally succeeded in what could not be done on the battlefield. The enemy has defeated the soldier. Choosing not to forgive, the soldier self destructs; he fails miserably and in essence surrenders to the very enemy he thought he had defeated. It is as if he threw a grenade at the enemy, who in turn pulled the pin and threw it back.

The sad reality is, as young warriors return from current war zones, it is the same ol', same ol'. History repeats itself as the warrior internalizes and finds a long, perceived list of people and circumstances to blame for his problems.

Forgiving is imperative! Based on the principles of the Lord's Prayer, "Forgive us our sins, for we also forgive everyone who sins against us,"[1] we must forgive. Unforgiveness will gnaw away at our very existence until we are destroyed.

Truth or myth, I know not, but a story has persisted for centuries... A murderer received an unholy and almost unimaginable punishment for his crime. The body of his victim was tied to the murderer: hand to hand, foot to foot, face to face. The perpetrator of the murderous act was confronted with, restricted by, and attached to the consequence of his behavior. Decomposition of the victim in such close proximity became the death knell to the guilty. He could not eat or sleep and was avoided by everyone, losing contact with friends and family. His body was soon infected by the putrid decaying flesh, which in turn, would ultimately cause his death...not unlike the cancer of unforgiveness, which destroys those who choose not to forgive.

It breaks my heart to see a young man who feels he has won the war only to lose his direction, his peace of mind and his family.

Conversely, one story comes to mind. It is the story of a warrior who is an excellent example, a shining star of a young man who discovered the power of forgiveness. A sergeant with the 10th Mountain Division of the U.S. Army stationed in Afghanistan was hit by a suicide bomber. Months earlier the armored vehicle in which he was riding was totally destroyed by a roadside bomb. Miraculously, he walked away unscathed. This time, the suicide bomber detonated approximately 36 inches from the door of the sergeant's up-armored Humvee. The powerful explosion was devastating, resulting in his being burned extensively and experiencing Traumatic Brain Injury (TBI). The TBI was so severe, that several years after the injury, he could not remember things as simple as what he had eaten hours before. He could not recall a conversation or even an assignment of duties just minutes after being told what to do.

As I worked diligently with the sergeant, helping him recover from his emotional and psychological trauma, I began to see small but promising changes. Recovery was beginning. Our most frequent conversations dealt with forgiveness. To forgive the suicide bomber would stretch him to a near-breaking point.

After all, the bomber was already dead. But the sergeant, intent on total recovery, proceeded to write a letter of forgiveness to the suicide bomber. Upon completing the letter, the transformation in the sergeant was as distinct as night from day. His memory has been restored, and the impact of TBI has been greatly reduced. His experience of post traumatic stress has allowed him to help others going through the consequences of war. He is one of the most outstanding young speakers of all of those trainees who have gone through the program at Eagles Summit Ranch. I truly believe the sergeant would still be enduring endless counseling sessions and making zero progress toward his recovery if he had not learned to forgive. He declares that two weeks at our program in Colorado did more for him than two years of counseling prior to his arrival at the ranch.

The secret of a warrior's recovery lies in the willingness to forgive. I learned to forgive. So must the warrior. So must you.

Forgiving does not imply forgetting. Forgiving is choosing not to remember the offense against the offender.

Forgiveness is not an option. It is a pleasure. The consequences of unforgiveness are far and away more serious and devastating than swallowing your pride and forgiving those who have scarred you.

Forgive and begin to live.

1Luke 11:4 *Today's New International Version*

*   *   *

Photos

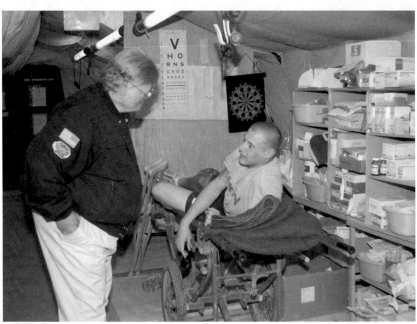

Dave and son Matt on tour in Iraq

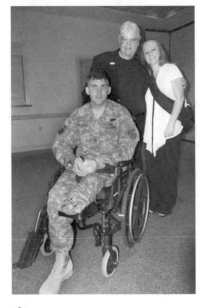

Dave receives Purple Heart thirty-four years after injury

Dave "Welcomes Home" Vietnam veterans

A Public School Assembly Program

Men's Convention at Razorback Stadium

Dave with Attorney General John Ashcroft

Bruce Wright, Lieutenant General USAF (Retired)

Benjamin Mixon, Lieutenant General US Army (Retired)

Brenda

From my friends

Dave Roever is an overcomer. For decades he has used his experiences to speak into the lives of young people teaching the values of responsibility, self-discipline and faith. After 9/11 he re-engaged in combat against the horrors of war where the enemy is often unseen. Our warriors are wounded physically, emotionally and spiritually. Follow my wonderful friend as he brings healing and hope through the pages of this book.

Robert W. Rufe
Captain, US Navy (Retired)

★   ★   ★

Dave Roever served his time in combat in Vietnam and since 9/11 has served alongside our service members in Iraq and Afghanistan. I spent Thanksgiving of 2006 with Dave in Northern Iraq visiting my soldiers. Everywhere we went soldiers flocked to Dave. He was a rock that they knew offered the firm footing of faith. I am proud to call Dave my friend and a fellow warrior.

Benjamin R. Mixon
Lieutenant General, US Army (Retired)

★   ★   ★

Dave is a true American Patriot putting GOD, Country and Family first in his everyday living. He is natural born leader with the highest degree of ethical, moral, spiritual and physical character. Dave's ability to organize, administer and relate to the needed treatment of returning wounded veterans is a treasure for the United States military and our entire country.

Robert E. Messerli
Major General, US Air Force (Retired)

★   ★   ★